Date

THE DEGRADATION OF THE ACADEMIC DOGMA

THE JOHN DEWEY SOCIETY LECTURE SERIES

The John Dewey Lecture is delivered annually under the sponsorship of the John Dewey Society at the annual meeting of the National Society of College Teachers of Education. This book is an elaboration of the Lecture given on that occasion. The intention of the Series is to provide a setting where able thinkers from various sectors of our intellectual life can direct their most searching thought to problems that involve the relation of education to culture. Arrangements for the presentation and publication of the Lecture are under the direction of the John Dewey Society Commission on Lectures.

WARD MADDEN, *Brooklyn College, City University of New York,*
Chairman and Editor

GEORGE E. AXTELLE
Southern Illinois University

VIRGIL CLIFT
New York University

ARNO A. BELLACK
Teachers College
Columbia University

GAIL KENNEDY
Amherst College

The John Dewey Society Lecture—Number Twelve

THE DEGRADATION OF THE ACADEMIC DOGMA: *The University in America, 1945–1970*

BY

Robert Nisbet

UNIVERSITY OF CALIFORNIA, RIVERSIDE

FOREWORD BY

Ward Madden

CHAIRMAN, COMMISSION ON LECTURES, THE JOHN DEWEY
SOCIETY FOR THE STUDY OF EDUCATION AND CULTURE

Basic Books, Inc., Publishers

NEW YORK   LONDON

FOREWORD

BY WARD MADDEN
Chairman, Commission on Lectures
The John Dewey Society for the Study of Education and Culture

N<small>O ONE NEEDS TO BE TOLD</small> that the university in America is in trouble. But it has remained for Robert Nisbet to demonstrate in this book how fundamental the trouble really is. He does so with the penetration of the historian of ideas, the special sensitivity of the sociologist, and the eloquence of a man who deeply cares.

The university is based upon an historic ideal that is incompatible with many of the forces of modernism. Worse, it is cooperating in nothing less than its own destruction, although its course is not irreversible. Professor Nisbet brilliantly shows that the university is today the last surviving medieval institution, and that it is now being destroyed by a secular Last Reformation, embodying social tendencies continuous with those that made the knight, the manor, and the universal Church obsolete. These forces are at work primarily within the university itself, in its own faculty, administration, functions, and organization.

The university is besieged by political movements on the right and left. It is lured by economic temptations flaunted by government and foundations. It is confronted by demands for kinds of social services that can be performed only by weakening the university's dedication to its own ideal. It is attacked by student revolutionaries, and despised by the general population for not putting down the revolutionaries. But as Robert Nisbet sees it, none of these are nearly so decisive as the university's own internal weaknesses, which have been long in the making, but at a sharply accelerated pace during the last two decades.

The trouble, according to him, is that the university has betrayed its own ideal. In doing so it has lost much of its vitality, its sense of community, and its authority. Its ideal is what he calls the "academc dogma." The heart of the academic dogma is the pursuit of knowledge *for its own sake.* Knowledge and the processes of coming to know are good in themselves, and the university, above all institutions, is— or used to be—devoted to them. To investigate, to find out, to organize and contemplate knowledge, these are what the university is all about. They constitute an ideal inherited from the Athenians, but first institutionalized in the form of the university during the Middle Ages.

The other basic element in the academic dogma is the ideal of teaching. If knowledge is good, helping the young to acquire knowledge and to learn the ways of knowing is also good. The university professor is not only a scholar; he is also a teacher. His teaching gains from his scholarship, and sometimes, but not always, the reverse is true. In any case, he is equally dedicated to both ideals; he is a teacher-scholar, not merely a teacher, not merely a researcher.

The forces of the Last Reformation working destructively within the university include, among others, a "higher capitalism," consisting of an entrepreneurial scramble by faculty and administrators for government and foundation money. This leads to the building of private empires in the form of research centers, institutes, and projects which, unintentionally or not, are antiuniversity in their effect. The Last Reformation includes, among still other things, a false individualism, which confuses the ideal of self-realization through pursuit of knowledge with self-realization through catering to a variety of personal and emotional needs which the university can make its central concern only by distorting its own ideal. Reformism, a false humanitarianism, and politicization weaken both scholarship and teaching. Robert Nisbet identifies these and a number of other degrading influences at length and describes their effects.

These temptations separate scholarship from teaching or dilute and bias scholarship by making it serve ends, however worthy, foreign to itself. The university is diverted from its own vocation. Like Augustine of the Confessions, the university finds the fascination of worldly experiences pulling it away from love of its true God.

At this point, Robert Nisbet will begin to sound to some readers like a neoclassicist, a humanist charging out of the Middle Ages armed with only a lance with which to joust with the windmills of twentieth-century industrialism, urbanism, and science, and only a sword with which to slay the dragons of population, pollution, prejudice, war, and alienation. For why can't the university, however rooted in antiquity, simply adapt to and be responsive to the needs of the twentieth century?

Nothing could be a worse misreading of this book. Robert Nisbet emphatically asserts that the university must *lead* the world into the twenty-first century. Its curricular structure and its scholarly interests must reflect the concerns, interests, and problems of the age. More than that, they must open up new issues, new areas of concern, investigation, and study.

However, the university's concern in these matters must *first of all* be scholarly, and only secondarily reformist or humanitarian. Humanitarian reforms are the products of knowledge and enlightenment, not the causes of knowledge and enlightenment. Robert Nisbet is himself a reform-minded sociologist, who has written and has personally worked on the political battleground in the interests of social betterment. But he believes that the university makes its best contribution to such ends when it sticks to its own distinctive function, which is the discovery and teaching of objective knowledge.

By why an academic *dogma?* Robert Nisbet speaks here, not as a perennialist who believes in unassailable absolutes, but as a sociologist who realizes that every human function has to be institutionalized in one form or another in order to be carried on at all. Every institutionalization of human activity is grounded on an unquestioned (not unquestionable!) faith which must be maintained in order to sustain the institution itself and the human function it embodies. If dogma seems the opposite of scholarship, which should be based upon the principle of open inquiry, then consider the case of science, an institution unquestionably devoted to inquiry. Every scientific inquiry is an act of faith in the worth of inquiry itself; every testing of an hypothesis is an act of faith in the idea that not only positive but even negative findings produce knowledge. Every inquiry must stabilize its premises in order even to locate its problems. These are part of the dogma of science, and in fact of scholarship in general, including the humanities.

And what about the ideal of the pursuit of knowledge for its own sake? This will jar many modernists. For them the right question is the Spencerian one of what knowledge is of most worth. And the right answer is also Spencerian—that knowledge which best serves the practical demands of the several departments of human living.

Yet there is an odd parallel between the classical ideal of knowledge as its own end and the formulation of John Dewey, who was second to none as a modernist, reformist, humanitarian. For Dewey the objective of life was experience. Experience is its own end, just as knowledge is for the classicist. The chief criterion of a good experience, said Dewey, is the extent to which it opens up possibilities for an ever deeper and wider range of experience. The classicist parallels this by asserting that a criterion of the worth of knowledge is the degree to which it opens up possibilities of discovering further knowledge. But for Dewey, experience *is* knowledge, and the only issue is whether knowing is a spectator or a participant activity.

That issue is fundamental, but it is not the one with which Robert Nisbet is concerned in this book. All he is arguing is that the crucial ideal for the university is the pursuit of knowledge as its own end. He does not deal with the underlying epistemological problem, nor need he, in order to make his point that the pursuit of knowledge in the long run results in the university's having humanitarian and reformist effects, far more productively than when it makes a direct attempt to perform these roles. The university casts its bread upon the waters, and its bread is knowledge.

And further, what about Robert Nisbet's vision of the academic community as elitist, aristocratic, hierarchical, with a strong sense of authority and superiority? Again, he speaks as a sociologist, not as a classicist. These are the sociological characteristics, acknowledged or unacknowledged, of every community, from the individual family unit to, yes, the purest forms of communism—the monasteries and the hippies' commune. That is, these characteristics are present if morale is high; if, in short, the community *is* a community. If the modernist spirit calls for democracy in the university, let it be noted that the sociological characteristics of community are not in themselves necessarily antidemocratic. They may or may not be. If hierarchical structure reflects differences in well-earned achievement, experience, and competence, if authority is the authority of knowledgeability, and if equality is seen as equal consideration of need and interest rather than as treating everyone in the same way, then no violation of democratic values is involved. If, in a mistaken democratization, the university loses its sense of authority, of excellence, and of leadership, then it is indeed doomed, just as Robert Nisbet fears.

PREFACE

THIS BOOK IS a very considerable enlargement of the John Dewey Lecture I was privileged to deliver in Chicago, February 27, 1970, before the members and guests of the John Dewey Society. I am grateful to the officers and members of the Society for the honor of their invitation and for the kindness and warmth of their reception of the lecture. To Professor Ward Madden of Brooklyn College I give particular thanks for his helpful and generous representation of the John Dewey Society during the period leading up to the lecture and for comments on the contents of the lecture that have appreciably enhanced this book.

Both the lecture and the book are in very large part a consequence of reflections and writings on the American university that began during the final years of a full decade (1953–1963) of administration in the University of California. Well before the onset of the student insurrections of the 1960s, it had become evident to me that since World War II changes had been taking place, more fundamental than any since the university first came into existence in America at the end of the nineteenth century as an adaptation of the traditional American college.

Part I of the book is an effort to describe, with warts included, the academic dogma and the academic community as these may fairly be said to have existed in America down until about World War II. I have tried meticulously to avoid any idealization of this dogma and this community, for none seems to me required. With all their failings, their proneness to a degree of academic torpor, their guildlike, sometimes aristocratic insulation from the hurly-burly of the wider world, both the dogma and the community aroused, as we know, very deep allegiances inside and outside the university. Plainly, such allegiances are wanting at the present time.

Part II is the real essence of the book: a description and analysis of the dislocating changes that have taken place in the American university since World War II. These are the changes, as I argue, that go far to explain the present agony of the university; the conspicuous loosening of the ties of community in the university; the all too evident weakening of the once proud authority that the academic dogma and community represented in America. I have held my analysis of the changes strictly to the American university. Possibly some of this analysis has relevance to the European universities; I cannot be sure. It may be said that I have exaggerated the concentration of the changes in the decade or two following World War II. Possibly this is true. The important point, in any case, is the intensity, the Reformation-like intensity, they indubitably took on in the period I am concerned with.

In Part III of the book I turn, rather synoptically, to, first, a few of the more significant proposals for the university now current in much American writing and, second, to some proposals of my own, requirements, as I believe them to be, of any revitalization of the university considered as *a setting for the discovery and critical examination of ideas, for the dispassionate and objective study of nature, society, and man, the whole undergirded by the functions of teaching and scholarship.*

I do not have to be told that such a conception of the university will be seen by more than a few readers today as falling within what a writer has recently called "the traditional antiquarianism of the academy." [1] For those who contemplate the university in the future as launching pad for permanent revolution in society, or as capstone of the research establishment in postindustrial America, or as adjunct to government, or as institutionalized patron of the arts, or as superhumanitarian to all of society's ills, contemplations I deal with in some detail in Chapter 12, the envisagement of the university as setting for dispassionate study and teaching of ideas must seem a pallid one indeed. So be it. Possibly the university, by virtue of an essentially aristocratic structure it acquired during the period of its birth, which was the Middle Ages, is as unlikely in the long run to survive the tempest-like ferocity of modernism as were, in retrospect today, the knighthood, the guild, and the manor.

Throughout the book I emphasize this possibility. Any assumption today of a built-in, necessary survival of the university in America is absurd. Technological society may have an abiding need for knowledge, but the university is far from being the only source of such knowledge even at its highest levels. The intellectual establishment is today large. There are other sources, needing only to be developed and multiplied. Inherently there is no more reason why the university should survive the kinds of change to which it has been so radically

[1] See Christopher Lehmann-Haupt, "The Historian as Activist," a review of Howard Zinn, *The Politics of History* (Boston: The Beacon Press, 1970) in *The New York Times,* May 4, 1970.

subject during the past quarter of a century than there was that the aristocracy and the guild should have survived the comparable changes that seized them at an earlier point in Western history.

What matters to society in any event, taking the long view, is not the university as such. It is, rather, the ideal to which the university has for nearly a thousand years given communal and aristocratic structure: the ideal of dispassionate reason, of knowledge for the sake of knowledge, of objective study of nature, society, and man. This ideal is, to be sure, a product of, not medieval society in the first instance, but of ancient Greece and those rationalists who, around the sixth century B.C., consecrated reason and objectivity as their predecessors had, for who knows how many ages, consecrated religious, political, economic, and self-survival partisanships.

I could be more respectful of most of the current repudiations of the university conceived as center for the dispassionate study of nature, society, and man if it were not for the fact that in these there is more than repudiation of the university: there is also repudiation of the very ideal of dispassionate reason. I do not see how civilization can very long survive that.

ROBERT NISBET

September 15, 1970
University of California,
Riverside

ACKNOWLEDGMENTS

Some of the contents of this book have appeared before, though in substantially different form. I am grateful to the American Council of Education, to Random House, Inc., and to the editors of *Commentary, Encounter,* and of *The Public Interest* for their kindness in allowing me to make use again of certain of the materials in the book. To the editors of *The Public Interest,* Daniel Bell and Irving Kristol, I offer particular thanks in this respect.

It goes without saying that over a period of thirty years there are many minds to whom I have acquired indebtedness for the conception of the university that is contained in these pages. To one of them, however, Irving Kristol, coeditor of *The Public Interest* and Henry R. Luce Professor at New York University, I am most deeply and directly indebted. Were it not for his own penetrating writings on the university in America and, even more important for me, the stimulus of countless conversations on the subject, it is very unlikely that I should ever have written this book. I take pleasure in being able to thank him publicly.

CONTENTS

THE DEGRADATION OF THE ACADEMIC DOGMA

INTRODUCTION

No ONE WILL MISS the indebtedness of the title of this book to Henry Adams, *The Degradation of the Democratic Dogma*. So far as I am aware, however, indebtedness does not extend beyond title. When Henry Adams and his brother Brooks used the word "degradation" in their writings, for the most part they had in mind a process in human history comparable to entropy in the physical world. Both the Adams brothers saw in the history of civilization an endemic running down of energy that was reflected, they believed, in an increasing dissolution of culture and of moral values in their own time. As is well known, their contemplation of the future of both American society and the Western world generally was one of considerable foreboding.

Nothing of that is to be found in this book. My referent throughout is the university in America: not the surrounding social order, not the American nation, not Western society. Whatever is happening to these larger entities is a matter I am happy to leave to others for judgment. I am even willing to stipulate for present purposes that these entities are undergoing changes of progressive character in which what I have chosen to call the degradation of the academic dogma is a necessary part. After all, there is no Golden Age known in history not based in some degree at least upon the dislodgment of old values and social structures. I am not suggesting that this is the case with respect to the American university and American society. How could anyone know? I am only emphasizing that it is a matter wholly beyond the purview of this book, which is confined to the university alone.

I use the word "degradation" in these pages solely with respect to the university, and I use the word in its strict and literal sense of a lowering of rank or office in society. That the university has suffered, during the past decade or two, a lowering of office in American society, a diminution of the esteem in which it was held almost universally until recently, seems to me no more than obvious. I do not say such degradation of role and function is either necessary or permanent. In the final chapter of my book I consider some of the proposals that have been put forth in very recent years for the revitalization of the university, and I offer the proposals that seem to me alone feasible in light of the nature of the historic academic community.

Most of the book is concerned, however, with the profound changes that have taken place in the American university since World War II. These, as I seek to show, are changes in the mission of the university, in its functions, in its structure of authority, and in its several roles and statuses.

I must emphasize strongly that I am *not* concerned in this book, except now and then in passing and in a very brief chapter toward the end, with the turmoil of the 1960s, with the student insurrections which, beginning at Berkeley in 1964, rolled across the academic landscape and succeeded as no other events in the history of the American university in obsessing academic and much public energy for nearly a decade.

To emphasize this in no way betokens lack of interest in or respect for the insurrections considered as historical events. Much is owing the student leaders of these insurrections in at least one sense. I do not think that we could have, any of us, realized how profoundly changed in structure the university had become, how deeply fissured, even fragmented, the academic community, had it not been for the relative ease with which bands of militant students succeeded in bringing to their knees not merely deans and presidents but entire faculties.

A philosopher of the nineteenth century—Nietzsche, I believe—once said: "When you see something slipping, push it." So might the leaders of the New Left on the campus have been warranted in thinking when, surveying the scene in the early 1960s, they began the series of onslaughts that were to include Berkeley, Harvard, Cornell, Columbia, Wisconsin, and Michigan, among the greater universities. It required freshness of vision perhaps but no great profundity to sense that the academic community had by 1960 been subjected to many of the same buffets of political and economic modernism that had in earlier centuries leveled the medieval knight, guildsman, patriarch, and bishop. Now, these same forces could be seen taking their toll from the equally medieval roles of professor, scholar, dean, provost, and chancellor.

I repeat, this book is not about the student insurrections of the 1960s. But it will aid the presentation of what I am concerned with in the book to ask this question: could the revolts of the 1960s, complete with all their depredations against library, classroom, laboratory, and study, have, under any reasonable assessment of the situation, occurred back

in the 1930s when the American campus was also radicalized?

The American university swarmed with radical students,
and also its fair share of radical faculty, in the 1930s—the
decade of Depression, fascism, and, as it seemed to so many,
of moribund capitalism. Both the Communist and the
Socialist parties were, by American standards at any rate,
substantial and well organized. Large numbers of students
were freely and proudly acknowledged members of these and
other radical political organizations. No one on the American campus then will have forgotten the hatred of the
political left for fascism in all its forms, for the economic
and political defenders of capitalism, imperialism, and of
what is today called the Establishment, and for the military,
widely believed by the left during most of the 1930s to be in
worldwide league against the Soviet Union and the revolutionary proletariat. One may speak without exaggeration of
a fully and genuinely revolutionary America in the 1930s.

But I cannot recall so much as an intimation of attack
from the political left *on the university.* Such attack was more
likely to come then from the right. There were indeed attacks
from the left on certain legislators, industrialists, and others
who, it was believed, were seeking to dominate the university. But not attacks on the university, its classrooms, laboratories, libraries, and faculty members. Not from the left. The
war against fascism and what was held to be the whole reactionary structure of capitalism did not then include the university, either in ideal or in actuality. This is, I believe, the
greatest single difference between the two radicalisms: that of
the 1930s and that of the 1960s.

How do we account for the difference in the two manifestations of radicalism so far as their relation to the nature, mission, and structure of the university is concerned? That question is, in a very substantial sense, the point of departure for this book.

I have made every effort to avoid captiousness or fault-finding in the pages that follow. I do not at any point seek to hide the profound respect I have, and have always had, for the university, considered as a setting for scholarship and teaching. No nobler institution came out of the Middle Ages. But my concern here is with describing the university, analyzing its nature and the changes that have taken place with such hurricane-like intensity within the university during the past quarter-century. If I do not seek to hide personal devotion to the university I first came to know in the 1930s—with Berkeley, Harvard, Columbia, Michigan, and Chicago among its greatest exemplars— neither do I seek to make personal devotion the cornerstone of my argument in this book. I like to think that one could be hostile to the very idea of the corporate guild we know as the university, as indeed some of the light and leading of the modern West have been hostile, and still concur with the basic outline of this book's argument.

For the prime point of the book is not that the traditional university was good, even though I believe it to have been good. The prime point is that a certain distinctive kind of community existed, with a distinctive dogma its core, and that this community and this dogma required supporting contexts: contexts which were largely destroyed during the period 1945–1960 by the economic, political, social, and intellectual changes I call the Last Reformation. One may choose to believe that the community, dogma, and contexts were obsolete and deserved to be destroyed in the interests of an ever more revolutionary democracy. If I oppose this view with every element of my being, I nevertheless respect it. The view is honest and coherent.

What is not honest or coherent, however, is the view that we may have the university, considered as intellectual community founded upon the rock of dispassionate reason, and also have, at one and the same time, as part and parcel of the same scene, the kinds of mission, activity, and role that have dominated the American university since World War II. I refer to what I have dealt with in this book as the university's roles of higher capitalist, chief of research establishment, superhumanitarian, benign therapist, adjunct government, and loyal revolutionary opposition. Each of these is doubtless a worthy role in society. What passes all imagination, however, is any conception of their being harnessed together in a single institution that continues to insist upon its aristocratic or priestly virtue in the cause of dispassionate reason.

We are like a religious monastery insisting upon all the affluence of a freebooting capitalism; an aristocracy masochistically tormenting itself with the slogans of revolutionary democracy; a community of pacifist contemplatives riding off in all directions at once to do battle with the enemy; an enclave of intellectual autonomy privileged to remake the entire social order through permanent politics and relentless humanitarianism. We declare ourselves an intellectual elite, fully entitled to aristocratic codes of honor and tenure, and at the same time hurly-burly of activities that at times even the surrounding social order seems too small to contain.

It is all a lovely fantasy. So must the feudal knight have

dreamed as he rode into the face of infantry and gunpowder.
So must have dreamed the guild masters in many a part of
Western Europe in the sixteenth century; their attire was
never more resplendent than just before they were van-
quished by the capitalist and the bureaucrat of the new
capitalism and the new nationalism.

I have not sought out villains in this book. I am willing
to stipulate that all the higher capitalists, men of power,
humanitarians, political intellectuals, and benign therapists I
deal with in Part II of the book are as chaste in attitude, as
dedicated in their way to the university, as the countless scholars and teachers of the traditional university were in their
way. Most of us in the academic world are all too prone to
seek out villains—in business, in government, in military;
everywhere except in the university itself.

But as George Meredith put the matter so nicely:

> *The wrong is mix'd. In tragic life, God wot,*
> *No villain need be! Passions spin the plot:*
> *We are betrayed by what is false within.*[1]

I do not hide in these pages my belief that during the
decade or two that followed World War II some values and
passions entered the American university that were very false
indeed to the underlying mission of the university and to the
essential contexts of the academic dogma and the academic
community.

[1] George Meredith, *Modern Love*, XLIII.

PART I

*The Nature of
the Academic Dogma*

1

THE LAST REFORMATION

ANY EFFORT TO UNDERSTAND the contemporary academic scene, its convulsive changes of the past quarter-century, its mounting conflicts of function, purpose, and allegiance, must begin with recognition of two facts of outstanding importance. Both are historical. The first is the aristocratic, even feudal structure of the university and also of its historic relation to the social order. The second fact, no less important, no less historical, is the deepening intensity and widening scope of the revolutionary change in modern Western society that, for want of a better term, we call modernism.

The university is, in a manner of speaking, the last of the great institutions formed during the Middle Ages: the last, that is, to suffer in full sweep the kind of changes and buffets that earlier were the lot of monastery, fief, guild, and parish. For many but not all medieval institutions these changes and buffets reached the height of their intensity in the sixteenth century during the Reformation. And it is indeed a Reformation that engulfs the university in America today.

It is surely evident that the university has become a battleground of interests, ideas, and allegiances in the same way the Church was in sixteenth-century Europe. Then, as we know, it was the assertedly corrupt character of the Church and its relation to society that aroused Zwingli, Luther, and Melanchthon.

Today, as events of the last decade have made only too clear, very similar doctrines are to be noted: doctrines of private economic interest among faculty members, doctrines of private political judgment among faculty and students alike within the corporate university, and doctrines of individual determination of truth among even undergraduate students. But today these doctrines have as their prime target, not the church—though I would not wish to suggest that the church, especially Christian, is without its own currents of revolt—but the university.

The belief that purity of faith and conscience, rather than works, including published works, is the proper road to salvation is as evident today as it was four hundred years ago. Then the Church was held to be the seat of corruption. Today, on all sides, the university is charged with the kind of society-sprung corruption and dishonesty that Luther and his allies saw in Rome. Now as then, the relation of man to institution, of institution to society, is a pressing one, with, however, the context academic rather than ecclesiastical.

I am not implying that only in the mid-twentieth century has the university known the impact of modernism. Changes of thought, curriculum, and theme have taken place throughout its eight centuries of history in the West: the impact of the Renaissance, with its joyous rejuvenations of classical, especially Greek, writers; the later impact of natural law doctrines; the critical rationalism of the eighteenth century;

the vital influence—but only slowly, reluctantly, accepted by
the universities—of the natural sciences; the burgeoning
professions in the nineteenth century and their largely successful efforts, especially in the United States, to become
elements of the university; the whole movement, of which
the Land Grant universities were leaders, through which new
and ever more vocationalized subjects were added to the university curriculum and through which the intellectual resources of the university were taken directly to the economy,
especially to agriculture. All of these are changes indeed in
that rather primitive curriculum that was the rock on which
a Bologna or Paris was founded in the early Middle Ages. I
do not deny them. Nor do I deny the conflicts within universities that not infrequently attended reception of new elements
in the curriculum.

But if we confine attention to the *structure* of the university
and to its principal components, changes are few and far between during centuries in which destruction or substantial
modification of such other medieval structures as aristocracy,
guild, village community, manor, and church was com-
monplace. From the thirteenth to the twentieth centuries, the
essential structural elements of the university have remained
largely the same, and almost as much the subject of social
honor today as they were then. The organization of the university into the two great divisions of faculty and students
and into schools, colleges, and faculties; the pervading hierarchy, not only from student to faculty member but, more
crucially, within faculty; the firm insistence upon faculty authority in matters of admissions, establishment of courses,
and, above all, in the granting of degrees, licenses, and certificates; the profound conception of the university as an enclave

of privilege and authority within the social order—that is, a *liberty,* in the medieval sense—with its correlative conceptions of academic freedom and tenure; the consecration of the university to teaching and scholarship within the learned disciplines; the primary of the role of the professor; even the academic gown, whether used for practical or ceremonial purposes—these are a few of what I mean by the structural and normative elements of the university. Very obviously, changes have been minimal and few in these respects. That is, until very recently.

For many centuries it was almost as though the waters of revolution were held back by powerful, if invisible, dikes when they threatened to reach the university. Not only did the proud and jealous citizens of academia fight against outside influences (sometimes to their own stultification), but so did almost all of the inhabitants of the world outside academic walls. No matter how willing the new men of wealth and of power were to see the historic positions of guild, parish, estate, and fief destroyed or weakened, it was, for a very long time, as though an invisible hand reached out from the twelfth century to repulse the forces of intellectual, economic, and political modernism when they threatened to touch the university. However quaint and anachronistic the lives of teachers and students within the walls might look to outsiders—a quaintness and anachronism almost perfectly reflected in the robes that became increasingly ceremonial ornaments—these lives, these roles, and the structure that contained them and the dogma that underlay them were largely left alone for some eight centuries.

Left alone until the present day. They are no longer being left alone, and it requires little gift of prophecy to be able to

see a future of almost limitless dislocation of academic structure, roles, functions, authority, and dogma. Such a statement
is made in no spirit of doomsaying or alarmism. The evi-
dences of dislocation already securely begun are too many
and too important to leave much room, it seems to me, for
any other kind of future. And, as I noted clearly in my prefa-
tory remarks, to say this is in no way to prophesy the decline
of knowledge, of culture, even of the contexts of effective
teaching. After all, the university as we have known it for
many centuries is only one of a number of possible ways of
meeting the problem faced by all societies: that of keeping
alive the springs and the contexts of the knowledge necessary
to survival; and also that of transmitting, through whatever
channels, this knowledge from generation to generation.

The evidence of comparative history leaves no doubt whatever that the university, much as we may cherish it, is anything but universal. Countless peoples, including some of the
most creative and intellectually advanced in history, have
met the problem of knowledge in ways other than that institutionalized in the university. Neither the greatness that was
Greece nor the grandeur that was Rome was based in any
way upon structures comparable to universities.

As one of the most distinguished historical interpreters of
the university, Charles H. Haskins, has written: "The Greeks
and the Romans, strange as it may seem, had no universities
in the sense in which the word has been used for the past
seven or eight centuries. They had higher education, but the
terms are not synonymous. Much of their instruction in law,
rhetoric, and philosophy it would be hard to surpass, but it
was not organized into the form of permanent institutions
of learning. . . . Only in the twelfth and thirteenth centuries

do there emerge in the world those features of organized education with which we are most familiar, all that machinery of instruction represented by faculties and colleges and courses of study, examinations and commencements and academic degrees. In all these matters we are the heirs and successors, not of Athens and Alexandria, but of Paris and Bologna." [1]

So too does that greatest of all historical interpreters of the university, Hastings Rashdall, emphasize the medieval source of the university in the West. "The institutions which the Middle Age has bequeathed to us are of greater and more imperishable value even than its cathedrals. And the university is distinctly a medieval institution—as much so as constitutional kingship, or parliaments, or trial by jury. The universities and the immediate products of their activity may be said to constitute the great achievement of the Middle Ages in the intellectual sphere." [2]

Note well this medieval source and character of the university. Without awareness of the continuing medievalism of university structure into the twentieth century we should not be able to understand the full significance of what is today happening to the university and, in all probability, will continue to happen in ever mounting intensity. For the moment, however, I want only to emphasize the fact that we err seriously if we make knowledge, its discovery and its dissemination even at the highest levels, synonymous with the university.

Nor has the university been the exclusive home of learning, research, scholarship, and creative intellectual discovery in

[1] Charles Homer Haskins, *The Rise of the Universities* (Ithaca: Cornell University Press, 1957), pp. 1–2.

[2] Hastings Rashdall, *The Universities of Europe in the Middle Ages* (Oxford: Oxford University Press, 1936), 1:3.

the modern West. A great many classics in all fields of
knowledge are testimony to this. Often, indeed, the university
could seem the home of ignorance, prejudice, mere ritualism,
to some of the light and leading of the West. The brilliant
burst of ideas we know as the French Enlightenment did not
take place within academic walls. More than a few fields of
learning, today integral parts of the university curriculum,
had to come into being not merely outside university walls
but under the lash of university scorn and contempt. If one
were to make a list of the hundred greatest works, including
scientific discoveries, in the realm of knowledge (which I will
of course distinguish here from works of artistic or religious
imagination), it is by no means certain that, even limiting
ourselves to the past three centuries, a majority of them
would be products of the universities. I should rather guess
the opposite; that a majority would *not* be such products.

I make these points about the university and its limited
relation to the discourse of knowledge not to derogate but,
rather, to set it in proper context for both past and present.
There are many attacks today on the university. There will
be many more in the future. Many of these attacks are and
will be based upon ignorance, bigotry, hatred of knowledge
in all its higher forms. But not all of them are or will be. In
the same way that a Gibbon or a Voltaire or a Bentham could
take a hostile view of the universities of their day for the
universities' ritualized resistance to fresh knowledge and fresh
ways of communicating it, so will more and more voices of
the near future echo this hostility.

They will echo it in the same spirit in which Gibbon, Voltaire, and Bentham themselves echoed, albeit in secularized
way, the still earlier hostility of the Protestant reformers to
the corporate Roman Church. Precisely as these reformers

found the corporate and hierarchical structure of the Church
a huge barrier to the individual's attainment of grace and
salvation, so have, and do today, other reformers and revolutionaries found the university with respect to cultivation of
mind and the attainment of true knowledge.

It is a mistake to think of the Reformation as something
that took place in the late sixteenth and early seventeenth
centuries. In a very real sense modern history, right down to
and including the present, has been one long series of intermittent Reformations. The zeal of assault that Luther and
Calvin applied to Church was applied by other reformers and
revolutionaries to other institutionalized products of the Middle Ages. The university is such a product, and I can think of
no better way, as I have already indicated, to assess the
significance of what is today happening in the university than
by likening it to that earlier phase of the Reformation in
which Luther and Calvin were protagonists.

The same fundamental combination of new wealth, new
power, and assertion of individuality we see in the Protestant
Reformation of the sixteenth century, we see also in the successive attacks mounted upon still other medieval institutions:
guild, village community, landed aristocracy, and so on. Today we see this attack mounted upon the last of the great
medieval institutions, the university.

Rashdall notes the striking likeness in the Middle Ages of
the guilds of scholars which were the universities, in our
sense, and the guilds of knights. "The original conception of
knighthood was the solemn reception of the novice into the
brotherhood of arms. The blessing of the priest was required
by the knight bachelor as the scholastic bachelor required
the licence of the chancellor. . . . Both of these great insti-

tutions arose from the transference to the military and scholastic life respectively of one of the most characteristic social and political ideas of the age—the idea of a guild or sworn brotherhood of persons following a common occupation." [3]

Modern history, Lord Acton once declared, is essentially the story of what has happened to medieval institutions and values. Nowhere is this observation more telling than with respect to the university, medieval to the core in its dogma and structure. Modernity has been anything but kind to the knighthoods—in all their guises and manifestations—that sprang into existence all over the European continent in the Middle Ages. What F. W. Maitland once wrote of the English sheriff could be applied as well to the medieval knight: that in his rise and fall can be epitomized all the major forces of modern European history.

As is only too plain, contemporary history is proving to be anything but kind to the role of professor, who is, after all, in academic dress no more, no less than a knight: a knight of the classroom, laboratory, and study, but not less a knight. He too is or has been the beneficiary of certain immunities and indulgences that the social order long since ceased to grant other knights, other craftsmen, other guildsmen. But I know of no better way of describing the contemporary Reformation in its impact upon the university than by saying that it is exceedingly unlikely that these immunities and indulgences will continue for much longer. As was the knight of combat several centuries ago, the knight of scholarship is today the victim of an erosion of role that threatens to make him obsolete.

[3] *Ibid.*, I:287.

2

THE ACADEMIC DOGMA

ALL MAJOR INSTITUTIONS are built around dogmas. So, for that matter, is social life generally. We could not live without dogma, which is no more than a system of principles or ideals widely believed to be not merely true or right but also beyond the necessity of the more or less constant verification we feel obliged to give so many other aspects of our lives.

"At different periods dogmatic belief is more or less common. It arises in different ways, and it may change its object and its form; but under no circumstances will dogmatic belief cease to exist, or, in other words, men will never cease to entertain some opinions on trust and without discussion." [1] So wrote Alexis de Tocqueville. Cardinal Newman was but echoing, and giving point to these words when he observed that men will die for a dogma who will not even stir for a conclusion. The word "dogma" comes from the Greek *dok* (*ein*) which may be translated as "seem good." Equality,

[1] Alexis de Tocqueville, *Democracy in America* (New York: Alfred A. Knopf, Inc., 1945), 2:8.

justice, freedom, democracy, all of these are dogmas for us today, just as the Godhead, the Resurrection, and spiritual grace were (and still are) dogmas for the Christian community.

To describe a belief as dogmatic does not necessarily imply that it cannot be "proved" through logic, reason, or evidence. No doubt each of modern man's dogmas—democracy, equality, justice, and others—could be so proved if we wished to submit it to critical or scientific scrutiny. A very considerable literature in the social sciences and moral philosophy seeks to do precisely this: "prove" on rational or empirical grounds that each of these is functional in light of man's real nature. A large literature in theology seeks to do the same with Christian dogmas.

None of this gets to the heart of the matter, however, or offsets the dogmatic character of the beliefs I refer to. The essential point is that irrespective of the possibility of their rational or empirical verification the beliefs are widely regarded as good or right without necessity of constant scrutiny. And, as Tocqueville wrote, adding to the words quoted above, no society can even exist, much less prosper, without such common belief. Nor can any individual. For if each individual was compelled to demonstrate and redemonstrate to his own satisfaction each of the propositions he lives by, his obligation would never end. As Tocqueville notes, man would exhaust his strength in preparatory demonstrations without ever advancing beyond them.

No community, no organization, no institution, then, can exist for long without dogma; without a belief or set of beliefs so deeply and widely held that it is more or less exempt from ordinary demands that its goodness or rightness be demonstrable at any given moment. The major revolutions in history, the major changes, for that matter, have involved dogmas. It is only when some long-held belief, such as in the infallibility of the pope in matters of faith and morals, or in the divine right of monarchical rule, crumbles before contrasting ideas that we may speak properly of fundamental change taking place in men's lives. New dogmas generally rise almost immediately—such as that of the infallibility or divine right of the people—but time is required for their wide acceptance, for their full attainment of the status of dogma. And the intervening period can be one of widespread doubt, disbelief in anything, and intellectual uncertainty. Then, as Tocqueville writes, men are no longer bound together by ideas but by interests; "and it would seem as if human opinions were reduced to a sort of intellectual dust, scattered on every side, unable to collect, unable to cohere." [2]

Dogma has been no less vital to the university during its eight hundred years of history in the West than it has to family, church, and state. And it is precisely with respect to dogma that the most revolutionary currents of change are to be seen at the present time in the academic world. A dogma that somehow managed to survive the first Reformation, the Age of Reason, the Enlightenment, the rise of industrialism, and the spread of political democracy, is today, for really the first time in the history of the university, under shattering attack.

What is the dogma that the university is built on? *Knowledge is important.* Just that. Not "relevant" knowledge; not "practical" knowledge; not the kind of knowledge that enables one to wield power, achieve success, or influence others. *Knowledge!*

[2] *Ibid.,* 2:7.

I don't want to idealize or otherwise distort here. Plainly, some types of knowledge have been more highly regarded than others, and one can write the history of the intellectual content of universities in terms of the succession of kinds of knowledge that have been regarded as important. Moreover, it is the very essence of the academic dogma that knowledge be thought of as stratified, with some types manifestly superior to others at any given point in time. One of the prime functions of the academic community has always been assessment through criteria peculiar to itself of the relative worths of knowledge.

Not the principle of utility or rationality, but dogma alone has made it possible, during the past century or two, for the Homeric or Chaucerian or Miltonian scholar to walk as tall on the campus as either the physician or the lawyer or the engineer. In fact, as we think about it, the former have been able to walk taller on the campus until perhaps a generation ago. Why is this? Why should an individual who may himself be unable to write a creative, respectable line of poetry or drama, who moreover lacks professional knowledge of anything that could possibly keep human beings alive during adversity, why should this individual, whose only glory is knowing perhaps more about Chaucer and also more about what others have known about Chaucer than most of us could possibly know, why should this personage have received the plaudits he so plainly has (that is, until very recently, at least)?

Obviously, I use the Chaucerian scholar as but a single example. Merely expand the significance of what I have said to the fields of history, philosophy, literature, classical and modern, or to any of the other disciplines within the university that have been, until recent decades, the most honored on the campus. Without exception such disciplines have depended upon, have had to depend upon, the dogma that whereas no one could easily prove (or, for that matter, would seek to prove) their instrumental value to either polity or personality, they are nonetheless important, even sacred. Or were!

Consider only the following anomaly. In the nineteenth century Parliamentary Commissions in England and federal legislation in the United States were required to crack the iron facades of the historic universities and colleges, thus permitting entry into the curricula of fields of study, many of them vital to human welfare, that academic hierarchies everywhere had stoutly repulsed. And even after fields such as engineering, agricultural science, and the human-welfare disciplines generally were admitted or, rather, forced their way with governmental assistance, they were, despite their manifest utility to human health and welfare, placed at the very bottom of the academic totem pole. Not even medicine and law, the two oldest of the professions, received much better consideration. In England not even a Parliamentary Commission would have tried to force law or medicine on Oxford or Cambridge. By comparison with the prestige carried by the metaphysician, the Shakespearian student, the historian of ancient Greece and Rome, that of the technologist—he for whom knowledge was, in Bacon's word, *power*—was miniscule.

The flavor of the anomaly is heightened when we realize that not only was this ranking of academic eminence to be found within the academy, where simple inertia might explain it even if vested interest is not invoked, but also in the lay world outside the academy. Is it not strange—except as it is seen through the prisms of dogma—that even among the nonintellectual, including the unlettered, the status of the philosopher and historian should have been for so many centuries higher than that of anyone with the skills or techniques that might have been counted upon for uplift of material conditions? And to a very considerable degree this is still true. No matter what recent events may have done to the status of the humanist within the university, as compared with that of the engineer or scientist, one does not have to go far outside the university to find that the prestige of such words as "history," "philosophy," and "theory" is still very high. If plumbing ever passes from its present system of apprenticeship to a college or organized curriculum, one may confidently predict high status for courses in the history and the philosophy of plumbing.

I do not mean to suggest that the humanities alone have been the beneficiaries of the academic dogma. Not by any means. It is worth remembering that the universities began in Europe around professional disciplines—theology, law, and medicine chiefly. But their place in the university, and the place of each and all of the disciplines that were to be added to the university in succeeding ages, was predicated on the vital assumption that each was a sphere of knowledge, and as such important. If I stress the humanities occasionally in this book it is chiefly because their historic status reflects, better than any of the "useful" disciplines, the profound role of dogma.

I can put this matter somewhat differently. Down until a generation ago in this country, there was a certain aura of the sacred surrounding knowledge and the man of knowledge, even, perhaps especially, in the eyes of the uneducated. It

was an aura that transferred itself to books, essays, and
articles—all vehicles of knowledge. (Older readers will perhaps remember the luster that once attended the book, before
that luster was extinguished in the flood of publication during
the past two or three decades, before books became, like
steel and automobiles, commodities.)

Historically, of course, there is nothing extraordinary about
the aura of the sacred that emanated from knowledge. The
academic dogma began, after all, in the medieval scholar's
study of the sacred: the sacred texts of Christianity foremost. The man of knowledge and his pursuits were sacred
because what he studied was by definition sacred. In due
time, however, the man of knowledge came to be interested
also in law and medicine, and then in a constantly proliferating body of ideas, texts, and theories. None of these later
subjects was in any sense sacred, of course. But in a very
important sense all of them, even the most secular, even the
most antitheistic, retained the aura of the sacred.

The early proposition (going far back in civilization) that
knowledge of the sacred is sacred became extended in time to
the proposition that knowledge, that is, genuine knowledge,
knowledge of a learned discipline, is itself sacred. Thus the
prestige of the classical scholar, the historian, the philosopher,
the philologist, and in time even the chemist and sociologist.
Except for these foundations of knowledge, foundations resting on the early belief that knowledge, true knowledge is
sacred by definition, the rather secure place of the man of
knowledge in the West would not have been gained. No
matter how much damage was to be done in modern centuries to the roles of guildsman, knight, and nobleman by the
storms of democracy and industrialism, the role of the man

of knowledge was left largely intact down to the present age. The scientist may today suppose that his prestige is the direct product of the practical things he does for mankind's welfare. There is something in this, to be sure. But in larger part, I think, his prestige is to be seen in lineal succession from the earlier, prescientific prestige of those other men of knowledge concerned with very different matters.

As is the case with all dogma, there is an evident, *aristocratic* character in the academic dogma, the dogma that knowledge is good. Later I shall say something about the aristocratic structure of the traditional university and of the roles that compose this structure. For now, however, I want to stay with the dogma itself. From the very beginning in the West, aristocracy has pervaded the realm of letters. There has never been any pretense of equality or democracy of ideas. Knowledge is sacred; knowledge also carries rank. I refer, of course, to knowledge as historically defined within the learned disciplines; defined in a sense that never included food-getting, house-building, and procreation, vital as these are to human life. From this origin has come the long-known, long-taken-for-granted fact that there is an inverse ratio between the prestige of knowledge and its practicality, its manifest utility.

First, as we know, theology was regarded in the Western university as the queen of disciplines. It was the idea that knowledge serves God, or rather our understanding of God, that first gave to knowledge its sacred place. Then, in due time, it was philosophy—above all, the study of the incomparable Aristotle but of many others too as their works became steadily more available in the West after the fall of Constantinople. Then, strongly rooted in theology and the works of the philosophers, the classics—meaning, chiefly, the learning of the languages of antiquity with their intellectual riches a byproduct. For centuries the so-called classical curriculum dominated the universities. Difficult as it was for the sciences to break into the curriculum, as I noted above, it was at times even more difficult for modern languages, literature, philosophy, and history to break in. But break in they did, for the most part in the late nineteenth century. All the earlier glory of theology and classics now went to them with the sciences more or less in the roles of bystanders; the professions scarcely less than outsiders. Such is, and has been, the power of the academic dogma.

Now let us turn to a slightly different aspect of the matter. I have emphasized knowledge, but in the university this knowledge has overwhelmingly meant a distinct type of knowledge. And to this type we give the word "scholarship." It is, at bottom, scholarly knowledge, not just knowledge in the fuller sense, that the university and the academic dogma have been built around. The recent history of the university makes this point worth a good deal of emphasis.

Here I must distinguish between two quite different types of knowledege in the West. Both have been honored; both go back to the very beginnings of civilization. The relationship between the two, and also the frequent conflict between them, are among the most important strands of the history of civilization.

In the first type, or tradition, of knowledge it is not so much erudition or patient accumulation of fact, insight, and interpretation that is at the core. Rather, it is purity of thought, brilliance of insight, and direct, even untutored, illumination of reality that is central. Charisma, not scholarship, is important. The whole prophetic tradition—a tradition that is by no means limited to the things immediately belonging to God—is formed around this conception of knowledge. It is truth, not learning as such that is involved here: knowledge *of,* not knowledge *about.* Hence the powerful influence in the world of knowledge of not merely a young Jesus striving to refute the scribes but also of a Socrates, a Plato. It has been often said that Plato could never have earned a Ph.D. for *The Republic.* Usually intent here is pejorative—to the Ph.D. But there is hard truth in it nonetheless. *The Republic* may be, as I believe it to be, the greatest book ever written in the West. It is knowledge, it is wisdom, it is brilliance, it is insight, it is revelation. But it is not scholarship! Nor, really, are the seminal parts of the work of Descartes in the seventeenth century. Descartes' *Meditations* and his *Discourse* are among the most antischolarly works ever written. For, again granting their knowledge, wisdom, insight, and so on, is it not true that Descartes himself declared his work antithetical to scholarship and learning by his insistence that knowledge, that is, *true* knowledge, could be gained by Everyman if only Everyman were willing to obey the simple laws of common sense? Down to this very moment this tradition continues in a host of spheres, including the New Left. Its pillar is the insistence that true knowledge, that is, truth, is available to the man of pure reason irrespective of his knowledge of texts, sacred or secular.

The second tradition, and the one that is central, of course, to the university, is more nearly Aristotelian than Platonic in its origins. It does not disparage reason, intuition, or common sense. Like the first, it aims at wisdom, truth, and enlightenment. But it differs from the first in the monumental empha-

sis that it places on cumulative knowledge, corporate knowledge; the kind of knowledge that is gained by men working
in terms of the works of others; the kind of knowledge that
declares the indispensability of texts, of sources, of the *ip-
sissima verba,* but also the indispensability of profound
learning regarding what *others* have said about these texts,
sources, and words.

It is easy to caricature, to belittle, the scholar's passion
for text and commentary. Many have done so in the past—
among them Rabelais, Francis Bacon, and Bentham—and
many more do so in the present age. At the heart of much
of the contemporary revulsion against the university is a revulsion against the kind of scholarship, always so near to
mere pedantry and rote, that the university has been built
upon for all of the centuries of its existence. This revulsion,
be it noted, as often characterizes university faculty members
today as students and intellectuals outside the academy. One
can understand, even sympathize with, much of it.

And yet what was distinctive, at bottom, in the great
European Renaissance was little more than this same passion
for scholarship, for text, and for commentary: for *classical*
text and commentary, particularly Greek text and commentary. What else, after all, were the great Scaliger, Erasmus,
and their innumerable contemporaries basically interested in,
but in demonstrating through their own scholarship the vitality of a tradition of thought that preceded, that helped shape,
Christianity. Scholarship was and is a mode of revolt against
the tyranny of certain kinds of creed and text. All modern
disciplines, including the sciences, arose in the first instance
in the West on the basis of a study of texts and commentaries
that had the university as its locus.

I hope it will be understood that I am not glorifying the second, the scholarly, tradition. Scholarship, for all the zeal and learning that may go into it, can be dull, stale, leaden, and profitless by any standard. Much of the scholarship that has disappeared through the centuries since the Middle Ages deserved to disappear. And no one acquainted with the history of European thought can do other than honor exponents of what I have called the first tradition: those who, like Descartes, the *philosophes,* the Philosophical Radicals in England, and many of the utilitarians, directed their energies to demolishing traditional scholarship and to clearing the ground and starting over, using chiefly the tools of intuitive insight, native acumen, and common sense. All of this is plain enough. Western society would be poor indeed were it deprived of the riches which have flowed from the genius of the first tradition. In it, far more often than in the second, has lain the vital impulse to change, to improve, to revolutionize the obsolete and corrupt.

But creative or sterile, leaden or buoyant, scholarship is basically what the academic dogma is about and has been about for close to eight hundred years. Its essence has been learning, erudition, and the influence these qualities have upon the development of mind and character.

One common error must be guarded against here. The university is not, and never has been at any time in its history, a retreat from the world. Very different are the monastic and the academic traditions in the West. From the very beginning the university, its faculty members, its students, and its graduates, has been in the thick of things—thick things, not thin ones. No retreatists or anchorites were those at Oxford, Bologna, Paris, and Salamanca in the Middle Ages and in succeeding centuries, who, as we know, loved strong drink, good food, buxom women in their rooms, and who were anything but averse to battle with representatives of both church and state.

What is much more to the point here, however, is the fact that from earliest times down to the present the university, and within it the academic dogma, were predicated upon a powerful sense of service to society. When Woodrow Wilson as university president revitalized American higher education with his words: "Princeton in the nation's service," he was doing precisely that, revitalizing, not creating something new in the way of a mission for the university. From the days when graduates of the universities went forth to serve Church and then State through their learning in law, law canon and Roman, down to the present time, the mission of the Western university has been conceived in terms of service, not monkish retreat.

But—and this is the vital point—such service was *indirect,* not direct. Only a few decades ago did there begin to take serious hold in the American university the view that its service to society, to government, and to professions and industry must be direct. Before that, going back to its very beginnings, the service rendered by the university lay not so much in what it did, but in what it was. We may think of the university, whether in its European, its English, or its American form, as the capstone of the process of socialization of youth that begins in family and school. Leaving aside the university's direct commitment to the scholarly disciplines, it provided a unique environment for young minds through their disciplined exposure to scholarship, manifest in the curriculum. There was, until relatively recently, nothing said

about life-adjustment values, about the nurture of individuality and personality. Unquestionably these were byproducts
of the university experience as far back as the twelfth century.
But the university pretended not at all to be an enterprise in
psychological values. It was an enterprise in scholarship.

Not that administrators and faculty members ever deluded
themselves that very many students would or should become
themselves masters of the craft of scholarship. The academic
dogma pronounced the things in a university curriculum important. Important in and for themselves. It followed, therefore, that these things were good for all minds in any way
disposed toward spending four years in the university.

Faculty members did not feel it necessary to try to adjust
each element of the curriculum to some imagined psychological need of the students. Undoubtedly faculty members
believed that there was a relation between the curriculum and
the social and moral, as well as mental, development of students. Not curriculum alone, of course. The genius of the
university lies in its combining of the intellectual with the
moral and social—in the academic community. I will come
to this shortly. My primary point here, however, is that
curriculum was shaped in terms of the criteria arising directly
from the learned disciplines themselves. Not from the criteria
of mental health. For centuries the classical curriculum was
the core of the university. It was succeeded, as it had to be,
given the advancement of knowledge, by still other curricula:
those in which the modern history and literature, the modern
languages, and, finally, the sciences, physical and social, were
prominent. But one and all these fields were chosen for
representation in the required curriculum, or for the ever
enlarging numbers of elective courses, on the basis of intellec-

tual-academic choices; not choices rooted in prior calculation of psychological and moral needs.

And yet for all the dominance of the academic dogma, for all the ascendancy of conviction that *it is good* for students to read Chaucer, Jane Austen, T. S. Eliot, *good* to study history, philosophy, sociology, and physics, *good* to accumulate knowledge in the learned disciplines, each of these *good in and for itself,* no one can doubt that a very real social and moral development took place in the student. There is vast testimony to this in the forms of memoirs, autobiographies, and countless other, generally less formal records.

And the university, for all its innate conservatism of structure, its dependence upon what I have called dogma, was notably the home of a substantial number of political, social, and intellectual radicals. If Oxford happens to be the university called the home of lost causes, it does not follow that a great many other universities lack claim to the title. Granted that many a buoyant and vigorous mind in the West, many a creator and radical, could not abide the corporatism of the university and cannot to this day. The university's history is still not without long and colorful chapters in intellectual heresy, innovation, and other departures from conventionality.

We must now turn to another and final aspect of what I have called the academic dogma: the overwhelmingly, almost totally, *Western* character of its intellectual content. From the beginning of its history in the twelfth and thirteenth centuries right down to the present moment, the university has been oriented intellectually toward the single, small, body of knowledge that first arose in that tiny part of the world we know as the Middle East; and, within this, chiefly from Israel and

Greece. From Isaiah and Plato down to contemporary offer-
ings in the humanities and also the social sciences is to be
seen a line of history unwaveringly Western in emphasis.

Even when, in the late eighteenth and the nineteenth
centuries, efforts began in the direction of comparative institutions, comparative history, comparative culture, these
tended, as we know, to be profoundly Western in their precipitating motivations and values. The so-called comparative
method—dear to the hearts of the founders of modern an-
thropology and sociology—was, in plain fact, a device for
arraying the non-Western cultures of the world in such a
way as to demonstrate the progressiveness of the West, to
show that such countries as France and England formed a
vanguard in the march of civilization. Not only university
thought but nineteenth-century thought in general in the West
was almost obsessively ethnocentric in this respect. We see it
in a Marx as well as a Herbert Spencer. But this Western
orientation I speak of, however great it could seem outside
the university, was the very essence of what lay intellectually
within the university.

It still is. I am aware of the tokenisms in very recent
decades—beginning just after World War II—by which tiny
morsels of intellectual food from non-Western parts of the
world were laid out on academic tables in this country. A
course in Swahili here, in India's languages there; a survey
of the history of Asia in one term here, an outline of African
and Oceanic history there. And so on. I have no desire to
disparage what has been done in American universities within
the past quarter of a century.

But one need only compare all that has been done in non-
Western spheres with what remains in the curriculum that is

solidly Western. Merely count courses in the catalogue: the number of courses in American, in English, in French or German literature, say, and those in the literatures of other whole *civilizations*.

The physical and biological (but *not* the social) sciences require exclusion here. It would be interesting to know how many of their envisagements of the natural world—the world that, by its nature, passes all cultural barriers—arise directly from indigenously Western presuppositions, from core ideas that are to be found in the West alone. We know, for example, how dependent the Darwinian statement of biological evolution was upon a pattern of ideas deriving directly from Aristotle and from Lucretius. Still, I will not seek to hide the fact that the curriculum of the natural sciences is, in a very correct sense, without national or civilizational boundaries.

One need only, however, recall the extraordinary difficulties the natural sciences had in the nineteenth century in winning a place for themselves in the universities. The center of the opposition to the sciences may have been in the classics, but let us not forget that the classics were the very heart of what I here call the university's Western ethnocentrism. Quite possibly the guardians of university portals in the nineteenth century foresaw the tensions that would be created in time within an academy Western to the core by the entrance of disciplines that could not, by their very nature, confine content to Western ideas, values, and facts.

The university, as I shall stress in the next chapter, is, and has been from its origins, primarily a guild. And it is the mark of every guild that it seeks to preserve the distinctive identity of its craft. And the craft of the university guild has been, for nearly eight centuries, scholarship: that is, scholarship in almost exclusively Western ideas and values. This fact is too often overlooked by commencement speakers and by others who should know better. They seek to find historic affinity between the words "university" and "universal." They cannot, for such affinity is not there. No one has emphasized more variously than Rashdall in his history of the university in the West the fact that, at no time, have these two words had functional relation.

Let us not conclude this treatment of the academic dogma without calling attention to the academic *faith* that has had to accompany it. I mean, of course, faith in the Western tradition: in the ideas, values, systems, and languages that belong to the tiny part of the world that is the promontory of the Eurasian continent known as Western Europe. Without faith, wrote Isaiah, the people perish. Without the faith I refer to here, the curriculum would perish; would have perished long ago.

A mighty act of faith is required, as one reflects on it, to sustain a curriculum century after century that scarcely deviates, and then under powerful pressure from the outside, from its commitment to the Aristotles, Augustines, Lockes, Rousseaus, Marxes, and John Deweys. I take nothing from the genius or stature of any of these. But I choose to attack, and hard, any supposition that our interest in these men, and their countless companions in the Western university tradition, rests upon our view of them *sub specie aeternitatis;* rests upon triumphant conclusion that, after careful comparison of these minds with others in other civilizations, they come out on top. It is faith alone that has enabled these men and their ideas to dominate large sectors of the university curriculum.

If an act of faith is required, century after century, to

commit mind and scholarship to the titans, to Aristotle, Augustine, or Leibniz, to Homer, Shakespeare, or Goethe, how vastly greater must be the faith required to support commitment to the large number of minor figures that abound in the pages of university and college catalogues. Does rational judgment really support the existence of a year course on the minor poets of the English seventeenth century when perhaps no course at all is given in the university on the major poets of the entire history of the Asiatic continent? Plainly not. Dogma and faith are required. I prefer these words to, say, "insularity" or "ethnocentrism."

Think only of the supreme acts of faith, and manifestation of Western dogma, required generation after generation to sustain history departments and their by now nearly ritualized curricula. I refer, of course, to their solemn divisions of courses into "ancient," "medieval," and "modern." *Whose* ancient, medieval, and modern? The West's, of course. All else is incidental.

But dogma and faith unsupported by the bonds of structure are, as comparative religion teaches us, notoriously fragile. And structure not served by some system of persisting authority is notoriously weak. And authority not undergirded by the sense of recognized function is notoriously tenuous. These are lessons derived not from sociology but from the wisdom of our grandmothers.

3

THE ACADEMIC COMMUNITY

WITHOUT DOGMA OF SOME KIND, a community is sterile. Without community, however, dogma is likely to be fragile and transitory. I shall use the word "community" in this chapter, indeed throughout the book, in the hard sense the word enjoys in contemporary sociology. Nothing mystical, arcane, or romantic is implied by my use of the word. I shall have reference here, just as Emile Durkheim had in his matchless study of religion, to the visible bonds, roles, statuses, and norms of hierarchy and authority that provide boundary and also reinforcement to what is spiritually or intellectually contained within the community.

The essence of religion, Durkheim wrote, is its emphasis on the sacred and its distinction between sacred things and those of profane or secular character. The function of the community, of the cult, is precisely the superintending of belief in the sacred and the differentiating between the sacred and the profane.

I have shown in the preceding pages that at the heart of the university in the West lies a dogma; one that declares knowledge sacred in and for itself. This is a declaration, as we have seen, that involves a kind of transposition of knowledge of the sacred. Enclosing the dogma, giving it both specific identity and necessary boundary, is a mighty faith in a certain, extremely limited (in a geographic and temporal sense) body of ideas and their makers. It is hardly too much to say that the university curriculum right down to the present moment resembles those ancient religions formed around pantheons; each replete with major gods and minor gods, all the objects of devotion and memory. For Zeus we may justifiably read Aristotle, and so on.

As faith surrounds dogma, so does community—in the strictly empirical sense—surround both dogma and faith. From the very beginning, as all historians of the university have stressed, the ties of community within the university have been very tightly drawn. The university began as a guild, one whose object was not combat, as was that of the guild of knights, or piety, as was that of the guild of monks, but, rather, scholarship. Scholarship in a writ that, however much it may have changed during the centuries, remained sacred, the rock on which curriculum was built.

We must look at the nature of community closely. So often today is this word a kind of talisman, a *summum bonum,* that we should be clear on what community is *not.* Community is not love compact, though love may exist within it as a sentiment. So, however, may the sentiment of hate. Hostility and hatred are never so intense as they can so often be found to be within the close ties of community.

Neither is community the direct, unmediated, consequence of any instinct for "togetherness" or "belongingness," to use two words with great current appeal in the popular magazines. I do not say that these qualities are absent. Far from it. I say only that no genuine, durable, and influential community has ever arisen on the base of these states of feeling. "Human beings," wrote Ortega y Gasset, "do not come together to *be* together; they come together to *do something* together."

Every community worthy of the name is built in the first instance around some *function*. As I have noted, this function may be good or evil, noble or base. Functions may range from crime or conspiracy to worship, scholarship, or child rearing. There is no end to the number of functions that have somewhere, sometime, provided the bases of communities. Nothing is so likely in the long run to lead to decay of community than the disappearance of the function that established it in the first place, or the failure of some new commanding function to take the place of the first.

Second, a community is strong in the sense of some transcending purpose, some ideal or ideals, or, as I have said in these pages, some *dogma*. It is not enough that a function be performed. This function must be converted, in the alembic of imagination and faith, into some deeply felt, profoundly held value. The function must—to return to the literal meaning of dogma—seem good.

Third, a community worthy of the name is strong in *authority*. This does not mean, not necessarily at any rate, the utilization of power or force. In fact, one of the best indices of breakdown of authority within a community is the turning to power or force in order to achieve objective or to fulfill function. Communal authority, whether in family, monastery, or university, is more likely to rest on some manifestation of consensus. Legitimacy, stated or unstated, is of the essence. At its most effective, the authority of a community over its members is unwritten, unprescriptive, and drawn from common experience, which is to say from tradition. But no one familiar with the behavior of communities will fail to emphasize the degree to which authority exists, and exists profoundly.

Fourth, a community is by nature *hierarchical.* Granted that persons are real to one another, that members come to be aware of each other in decidedly personal, rather than impersonal, terms. The fact remains that roles and statuses are distinct. One is a member of a community as father, mother, priest, soldier, student, or professor, as well as human being or person. His identity in the community is inseparable from certain norms, which are the norms of the whole community. And it is impossible to array all of these roles on the same line of equality. The father has a certain role-superiority to son; the professor has a role-superiority to student; the knight to squire; the master to journeyman or apprentice. Hierarchy is as constitutive a trait to community as is function or authority.

Fifth, a community, as distinct from a mere aggregate of individuals, is strong in the sense of *solidarity,* of the normative superiority of the whole over any one of its members. In a community it is almost instinctual for members to say "we." And one may trace the phases of dissolution of a community in the rising number of instances in which one is more likely to say "I" than "we." Corporatism is at premium; individualism at near nullity. The sense of duty is strong—duty to role, which is itself defined by the community, duty to the norms of the community, duty to the community itself.

Sixth, it is impossible to miss in any genuine community a strong sense of *honor* or *status*. It is a sense that does not merely distinguish itself from material or utilitarian or pecuniary interest; it actually subordinates these, treats them disparagingly, even contemptuously. In the community of blood, kinship cannot be assessed in terms of either material or pecuniary interest. In the community of combat, as in the medieval knighthood, one fought in terms of the duty that arose from membership in community. And in the traditional community of scholarship, in the university, one prided himself indeed on an aloofness to the kinds of material or dollar interests that actuated businessmen. One was true to himself as scholar or teacher, just as one was true to himself as father or as craftsman. "Cash" and "cash-nexus" were terms of disparagement. (And still are in the academic communty, even by those who not only do good but do well.)

Finally, one tends to find in any community a striking sense of not merely distance from the surrounding world, but of *superiority* to it—measured in terms of what one's own community does and is and what the rest of the world does not do and isn't. As is well known, one can find this sense of collective superiority even in communities of homosexuals, narcotics addicts, and delinquents. We are told that in the Middle Ages even beggars, pickpockets, and prostitutes—all communally organized, of course—possessed this sense; able, as Villon sang, to look down upon nobles and kings. Today in the so-called community of poverty there is not lacking, at least in some degree, a certain contempt for those of us who lash ourselves with the Protestant Ethic and seem never to stop running.

These, I think, are the crucial attributes of community. I

repeat, they do not predispose men within a community to love one another ardently, even to like one another. Hostilities and hatreds can sometimes be heroic. Only in those looser, more impersonal, and frankly individualistic types of association in which contemporary society is so rich are we likely to find that constant state of mind which is a little less than love and a little less than hate. In community, if it be true that men can love one another intensely and devotedly, it is equally true that they can hate and despise one another. No one who knew the academic community as it was, and no doubt still is—despite the sterilizing effects of modernism on the contemporary university—can doubt that enmities of a fiercely personal sort could continue for years, even decades. When one began teaching at a university almost the first things one learned were the hostilities that divided this or that pair of faculty members, the rooted conflicts of objective that divided this department from that and, every so often, the conflict that engulfed an entire faculty when some major issue arose. As we know, conflicts were also to be found between faculties and their deans or presidents. It would be a gross disservice, false indeed, to imply that the academic community was free of internal conflict or that it was surcharged with feelings of radiant good will.

It is, however, the nature of a community, properly so-called, that unlike certain other types of association, it can endure these conflicts, contain them, for very long periods of time without the fundamental structure of the community being seriously affected. One could make out a case, I think, following Simmel, for the actual strengthening of the bonds of a community as a result of these internal conflicts—not to mention the more overt ones between community and surrounding society. What eventually fragments or destroys a community is not conflict in the sense I have just cited but, rather, those conflicts which strike directly at the central purpose of the community, the kinds of conflict that occur when, as the result of intrusion of new goals and objectives, or the impact of external events and forces, the very dogma underlying a community is eroded away. I shall come to this kind of conflict shortly. It is at the heart of the degradation of the academic dogma. But first something must be said about the nature of the *academic* community.

We need not repeat what has already been emphasized about the underlying function of the academic community, which was universally regarded as the discovery and the teaching of knowledge as this knowledge was made manifest by cumulative scholarship. Nor need anything else be said about the dogma on which the academic community rested, which was the dogma of knowledge within the learned disciplines, the dogma that declared knowledge to be good in and for itself, irrespective of any discernible practicality, relevance, or demonstrable capacity for binding up wounds to the ego or fractures of one's identity. But something should be said, however briefly, about the specific character of community as it existed in the traditional university.

The essential authority of the academic community arose directly from the faculty itself—from a faculty uniformly engaged in the single function of teaching-research. I am not forgetting the lay boards of trustees which could occasionally dominate and temporarily rupture the academic community, nor the capacity of an occasional president or dean, such as Eliot at Harvard, Hutchins at Chicago, or, earlier, Woodrow

Wilson at Princeton, to try to work his will. But anyone who has studied the careers of these men will know the immense personal power and skill required by an administrator to accomplish his reforms. Nothing, as was well known in the traditional academic community, could so quickly bring out the spirit of "togetherness" in a faculty as assault upon its curricular *mores* by some independent and bold dean or president. Trustees and presidents well knew faculty authority.

One could in fact assess the widely recognized quality and prestige of universities by the degree to which faculty authority prevailed in matters relating to curricula, admissions, and the granting of degrees. At a Harvard, Chicago, or Berkeley it was inconceivable that any but faculty members would pass with finality upon whether a certain course was to be offered, whether a new curriculum was to be established, and on which students were to be admitted, by what criteria, and which students were to be granted degrees. To presidents and trustees were allowed the right to confer *honorary* degrees, but that was the sum of administrative authority in a matter that was properly deemed vital to the faculty and its authority.

There were inevitably other areas in which faculty authority extended itself and could become formidable. Privilege and tenure matters, of course, along with those of policy. Above all, however, authority over appointments and promotions within the university. I say "authority" advisedly. Only the president and trustees had the *power* of appointment and promotion in the American university. And sometimes use of this power was necessary in the interests of either equity or infusion of new blood. But in the good universities

in the country, the power of appointment or promotion—
whether within academic ranks or from academic ranks to
deanships and provostships—was rarely used except in con-
cert with faculty authority in the matter. Nothing was more
vital to a faculty than that it be consulted regularly, and its
judgment followed in all except the smallest number of
cases, when it came to appointments and promotions.

One is struck, as one looks back on the histories of the
best colleges and universities in this country, by the rarity of
overt conflict between faculty and administration, between
faculty and trustees. As Seymour Martin Lipset has acutely
noted, one could for a long time assess the academic quality
of a university almost perfectly by the degree of trust that
seemed to exist between faculty and administration. To be
sure there was, and had to be, vigilance on the part of the
faculty; and there was not seldom at least a modicum of
effort on the part of the administration to slip through the
interstices of faculty authority. But except during times of
transcending crisis—such as the conflict between Woodrow
Wilson and the faculty at Princeton, between Robert
Hutchins and the faculty at Chicago, and the celebrated
loyalty oath controversy at Berkeley—there was a kind of
tacit agreement under which the administration administered,
the faculty taught, did research, and governed! Governed,
that is, academically.

This last calls for special notice. I think it likely that
a great deal of the faculty's very great authority in the best
universities flowed from a certain saving sense of what
matters its authority should cover and what matters it should
stay completely away from, leaving squarely to the administration without faculty interference. Martin Trow has sug-

gested that a kind of unwritten pact existed between the faculty and administration under which, in effect at least, the administration agreed to stay clear of all fundamental academic matters involving authority, and the faculty agreed to stay away from supervision of extracurricular discipline, residence-hall life, athletics, and so on. Nothing, as we know, can so quickly weaken, even render ineffectual, a vital authority as the effort by some of its wielders to extend it indiscriminately. Inevitably a certain dilution of the core-authority must take place through distraction from the central ends around which it is built. In recent years, as I shall note in more detail below, the faculty has lost a good deal of its basic authority over curriculum and research, even appointments, through the sheer extension of this authority into such basically unimportant spheres as dormitory supervision and student pranks and delinquencies.

Let us turn to academic hierarchy. Few structures have been more stratified, more sharply layered in distinct ranks, than the academic community. I do not question the liberality that existed, even the democratic thrust of its emphasis on ideas and reason. But hierarchy was the essence of the community, from freshman to senior among students, from instructor to professor among faculty. And what gave direction, meaning, to this hierarchy was the academic dogma alone. One's status position in the university community was fixed more or less exactly by what one had managed to demonstrate in the way of teaching effectiveness and in scholarship. The academic community prided itself, as we know, on its rigorous exclusion of all other criteria in the fixing of a man's rank. So too among students was the academic dogma final in the fixing of position, in the advancement through successive classes to completion.

Gerontocratic philosophy tended to dominate. Not often did assistant professors rise in faculty meeting to joust with their elders. All faculty members were equal in theory but, quite plainly, some were more equal than others. There was, to be sure, special place accorded the president. To this position the faculty commonly rendered very considerable respect, as it did indeed to each of the other administrative positions in the community, including that of department chairmen. But academic criteria dominated nevertheless. Even the president was referred to as *primus inter pares,* a phrase right out of the Middle Ages, and as reflective as any phrase one might come up with of the reality of the situation.

Needless to emphasize, students were under the almost total authority of faculty and of administration. Theirs was to do or depart, not to advise, lead, guide, or govern. The authority of the faculty member over students in his classes was absolute and without appeal in academic matters. And the authority of the corporate faculty over the entirety of students was equally absolute in admissions, programs, and degrees. The power of expulsion from the university by administration for moral delinquencies was matched by the power of the faculty to dismiss for academic delinquencies. Students today fighting for participation on faculty committees and councils, even for membership on boards of trustees, have every right to declare the traditional system one of almost total deprivation of student rights, student participation, and student will. The one question is: To what effect?

So too do assistant professors today have every right to pronounce the traditional academic community an authoritarian gerontocracy. For the qualities in which the young tend to excel—energy, originality, brilliance—were not crucial to the traditional academic community when it came to either advancement up the academic ladder or to participation in the powerful councils of the organized faculty. I do not say that the university was hostile to these qualities of youth. It was anything but hostile. In its way the university honored them. But only in their place. And their place was generally regarded as being properly in the classroom, in the library or study, and not in the ranks of either the full professors or the councils of those entrusted with the government of the faculty and the students. What did count heavily in the traditional academic community, so far as high status was concerned, was wisdom and experience—however variously these might be defined, however unrecognizable they may have been in certain individuals of advanced age and status. Not even the Congress of the United States is more seniority-ridden than was the old academic community. As I say, one can easily understand revolt against the university today by students and by younger faculty members. But, again, to what effect?

Now let me turn to two final qualities of the academic community: the sense of *honor* that is, as I have stressed, an intangible but potent element of any community, including the community of poverty or any community of thieves or pickpockets. And second the sense of proud *superiority* to the rest of society. Each is, to be sure, a relative term. But no genuine community can be understood without reference to each.

One could feel the sense of honor throughout the academic world. Granted that it was all too easily exploited by surrounding society in that it was made a substitute, so to speak, for monetary reward. But that is the essence always of honor. It is an attribute regarded by members of the community and by the social order outside as inhering in a given occupation or role and that cannot be, by the very nature of the attribute, measured or compensated by money or material reward. Indeed the very lack of money—or, at very least, concealment of money and its benefits—is one of the historic signs of honor. The ambulance-chasing lawyer may earn vast sums by comparison with the salary paid a Supreme Court justice. No one argues that such a justice should be paid the equivalent of what large numbers of lawyers earn annually. Honor inheres in the Court in a way that renders thought of assessment in dollar terms faintly grotesque.

So with the traditional academic community. Its members did not despise money. The academic community was built upon no vows of either poverty or chastity. Still, as in all aristocracies, whether of birth or learning, there was a certain, noticeable, disdain for the businessman, for the individual whose sole mark of distinction was the amount of money he had earned, for all, in short, in whom some charisma of spirit and ancestry (even if bookish ancestry) could not be found. As I recall vividly, nothing would have so offended a bona fide prince of learning as to have been mistaken somewhere for a mere man of trade and commerce.

The stringency of the academic code of honor, and also its aristocratic roots, was to be seen in the disdain that the traditional academic community tended to feel for the faculty member whose writing was largely confined to textbooks. To undo the possible stigma that came from authorship of a successful, that is lucrative, textbook, one had to prove his mettle in an extraordinary display of the unbought graces of pure scholarship and science. How different it is today!

So too did one find the notion of academic honor in the innumerable mores pertaining to conduct within one's university and within one's academic discipline that stretched beyond the campus. Ambition was respected; never competition. No one was so foolish as not to know that a given scholar's life might pivot upon his desire to excell some colleague in terms of renown and salary. But no one was so foolish as to ever let this be known through his own overt expression. Finally, honor, as a motivating concept could be seen in the sphere of *academic* honesty and morality. One might be a notorious breaker of all the Commandments and survive, provided only that he avoided breaking the academic commandments against *scholarly* stealing and related forms of academic delinquency.

It is worth emphasizing here that in one sense even students participated in the honor that inhered in the academic community. Hence what has been known in the United States for many decades, going back indeed to the nineteenth century, as the "honor system." Inasmuch as no gentleman, by definition, cheats, steals, or lies, students (being gentlemen by definition) were on their honor not to do these things. Where the honor system prevails (it is today nearly gone in the United States except in a tiny number of small private colleges and a handful of universities—the latter chiefly in the South), the student is on his honor not to cheat, steal, or lie. Correlatively, the administration of the university does not run the risk of sullying this honor by snooping, prying, or policing. That is, in these academic matters alone. Drunkenness, wenching, gambling, rowdy behavior, all of these are well within the province of the gentleman, as historically defined, and in these matters—since lay boards of trustees tended to forbid them sternly—students were not on their honor, would not have wished to be, and extracurricular life could be seen, therefore, as a perpetual contest between the students and the officers of administration, with no holds barred!

A curious reversal of this whole arrangement began to take place two or three decades ago. As more and more students, especially the good ones, became incensed by the all too common instances of cheating in examinations—gentlemen or no—they demanded on many campuses an end to the "honor system" as it applied to curriculum, but, in rising volume, began to demand the establishment of an honor system with regard to personal lives and to matters that had been historically dealt with under the concept of *in loco parentis*. Today, for the most part, the honor system exists in neither sense. In academic areas, such as examinations, surveillance of almost electronic sophistication is standard. And in the nonacademic areas—housing, sex lives, drinking, and so on— the concept of honor system is irrelevant simply because by now these areas are almost everywhere deemed to fall under *laissez-faire, laissez-aller*.

It was the sense of indwelling honor in the traditional academic community, of social status arising directly from the academic dogma, that inevitably led to another mark of the community, the mark of superiority to the rest of the world. I am not accusing members of the academic community of either snobbishness or superciliousness. I rarely if ever saw these—except as they not infrequently may have been seen among academics themselves, that is, from one to another— within the academic community. But, as I noted above, this sense of superiority, however genteelly muted it may be, is a hallmark of any tightly knit community that is forced to survey itself with respect to the rest of the world. It is to be found within communities of the delinquent, the conspiratorial, even of the generations-old impoverished, as well as among guildsmen, knights, and monks. Certainly, one found this sense of superiority—a superiority rooted in the academic dogma—among the teachers and scholars of the traditional academic community. At its best it was pride. At its worst it could be, and was, arrogance.

There are two final notes that should be made about the character and context of the academic community. I hesitate to call them attributes or to place them in the same class of importance of those I have just described. They must nonetheless be mentioned.

The first is the considerable degree of isolation, immurement, call it what we will, of the academic community. It tended to be a world of its own for the overwhelming majority of its inhabitants. This is, of course, a characteristic of nearly all genuine communities, and we can see it brought to high intensity among academics. Rarely did members of the academic community mingle with either the business or working classes of society. Had one made a study of the acquaintance and friendship networks of members of some random sample of the academic community, he would have found almost total self-containment. Academic people and the people who occupied the other spheres of society rarely saw each other despite the effort in some places to establish "town and gown" clubs. Indeed, the higher the prestige of a given university in the academic world, the more probable total segregation was. To the president was left the vital matter of translating the purposes of the university to the wider social order.

The second quality may be called autarky, though it is clearly relative here. After all, income for the academic community came from the outside, through taxes, endowments, and other contributions. Still it is worth emphasizing that virtually all members of the academic community were dependent on it: *economically* dependent on it. With the fewest exceptions (I knew of perhaps half a dozen on the substantial Berkeley faculty of the 1930s, no more) members of the university drew not merely their livelihoods but their research money, their travel assistance for attendance at professional meetings, their clerical and secretarial assistance, and their other academic perquisites *solely from the academic community itself.*

I stress this last point. For, there is nothing like direct and perceived economic interdependence to stimulate and feed the sense of social and psychological interdependence. And, as I wish to stress in the next section of this essay, it was precisely the substantial rupture in the economic base of the traditional academic community that led in time to all the fragmentations and atomizations that are today such vivid social conditions of the community. Just as the Reformation in the Church in the sixteenth century may be traced in so large degree to economic perturbations of European society, so may the contemporary Reformation in the American university.

This, then, is the academic community and, undergirding it, the academic dogma on which the university was based as an institution. I have made every effort to avoid bathing it in nostalgia or romance, beyond admitting my own fondness for it. If by current standards the traditional academic community was quiet, so was it—also by current standards—frequently lethargic. If there were the titans of intellect *cum* scholarship who produced enduring masterpieces of literature as well as of knowledge, there were considerably more who spent lifetimes embroidering their doctoral dissertations. If there were teachers whose fame continued long after their deaths, there are a good many more in the lecture hall or seminar room who taught with tedious didacticism, those, it was said, who could kill a classic at fifty paces with the lethal literalism of their approach.

I have stressed the degree to which the academic community could become stodgy and torpid as the result of its isolation from broader currents of life and thought. From Edward Gibbon in the eighteenth century down to such minds as H. L. Mencken, Albert J. Nock, and Edmund Wilson in our own age there are vivid testaments to the inability of many vigorous, buoyant, and original minds to tolerate the closeness of atmosphere one found in the academic community. And, as I have also stressed, the academic community was, from the point of view of the young—no matter how able—scarcely more than a gerontocracy; at best a republic; never a democracy. And from the point of view of the student, the academic community can only be described as authoritarian and utterly paternalistic.

None of this large side of the university is to be questioned. Neither, however, can we question the truth that within the university there flourished, for some eight centuries in the West, a unique fusion of the quest for knowledge through scholarship and the dissemination of this knowledge through teaching. Nor can we question the high esteem in which the academic community was generally held. The eagerness of towns, from twelfth-century Bologna and Paris all the way down to twentieth-century society, to become the sites of universities shows clearly enough that persisting esteem, no matter how difficult townspeople could find brawling students and often arrogant faculty. Nor can we question the immense appeal the university had for students of the upper and middle classes. Few excitements were greater in late adolescence than that of, first, admission and, second, graduation. American society, unable to enjoy the kinds of ceremonial display to be found in, say, Catholic Italy or in royal England, found a great deal of compensation in the annual commencement ceremony in which, through gown as well as ritual, incantation, and investiture, nearly a thousand years of the Western tradition was unfolded before them.

Nor, finally, can we question either the fact of the academic community itself or its remarkable persistence through the centuries, with structure largely unaltered. The academic community was held together by common function, by common allegiance to dogma—the dogma of scholarship—by common authority, by a deeply rooted system of hierarchy, and by common sense of honor and of the superiority of the academic dogma and of the academic role to most of the rest of the social order. And as for the persistence of the university through historical time: one need but note the striking structural and role similarities of that university in medieval Europe that Hastings Rashdall has sketched for us in matchless detail and any of the great universities of the American twentieth century.

❧ 4 ❧

THE YIELD OF ACADEMIC
FEUDALISM

I MEAN BY THE TITLE of this chapter nothing more than two striking and very fundamental attributes of the academic dogma and the academic community: *tenure* and *freedom,* taking each in the distinctive sense it possesses in the university and college. Such is the importance, and also the widespread misunderstanding, of each that I have felt it worthwhile to give them separate treatment in this chapter.

Tenure and freedom; yield of feudalism? It may be thought that I write with tongue in cheek. Are these not perquisites of modernism, of humanitarian democracy and individualistic liberalism? Does not each have clear roots in this country in the Declaration of Independence and the Bill of Rights? They do not. Both spring from the profoundly feudal character of the academic community I have just described. Each is closely, even functionally related to the concept of honor that I dealt with as a distinctive attribute of the academic community. Both concepts, tenure and freedom, are lineally descended from that most cherished of feudal legal concepts, *liberty*. A liberty, in the medieval sense, was no more than an enclave, a corporate autonomy in society that deserved its own freedom to act in proportion to the honor of its mission, the protection it gave to its members, and the importance of its contribution to society.

It is important to mark carefully the special characteristics of academic freedom and academic tenure as these have existed—in whatever degree of substantiality and of explicitness—for a long time. Neither is likely to last a great deal longer in the American university. For, as I shall make clear in the rest of this book, the university has become too much like the larger society around it in its values and motivations for members of the larger society to endure cheerfully the continued spectacle of differential privilege accruing to members of the academic world. It was one thing to tolerate the *mystique* of tenure when the economic lot of the professor was no better than that of the clergyman. It is something else when the professor has become a member of the affluent society. It was one thing to tolerate the idea of academic freedom when it meant only a physicist's or sociologist's right to write and teach *as a physicist or sociologist*. It is something very different when the idea is applied indiscriminately to all aspects of existence and to the rawest student as well as to the most learned scholar.

Just as the concept of honor—in the sense I used for this word in the preceding chapter—has already disappeared, so will the related concepts of tenure and academic freedom. It is therefore useful to examine both of them, however briefly and inadequately.

Just as the belief in a special honor inhering in academic society prevailed widely among members of the traditional academic community, so did the belief in rights to a special kind of security of position and a special kind of freedom of thought. Despite the astute efforts of many academic spokesmen to persuade the public—and other parts of the larger intellectual establishment—that academic freedom is no more than a simple derivation from the Bill of Rights, it is anything but this. It is instead the declaration that the university or college is a *liberty,* endowed with certain rights that do not belong in a business enterprise or government bureau. When medieval lawyers referred to a "liberty" they had in mind one or other of the corporate groups, usually chartered, that could claim autonomy in society and, within this autonomy, freedom of action by members of the "liberty." The medieval university was a "liberty" in this sense; hence the battles by faculty and students to preserve its autonomy against town and church.

Hence too the frequent, and still passionate, battles of faculty members—and also students—in our own day—to fortify their claimed rights and prerogatives against the kinds of subjection to criteria of efficiency and productivity that are the lot of other workers and professionals in our society, including those in other sectors of the intellectual establishment. Only in the academic fastness that is the university does one find the stout insistence upon a degree of freedom of work, action, thought, and attitude that no member of the media, or the legal and medical professions, or the governmental intelligentsia would dream of claiming.

But, as I say, we miss utterly the nature of this claim to the special kind of freedom that is contained in the concept of academic freedom if we do not see its once-unquestioned linkage to the other concepts of honor and tenure. Taken together they are no different from the yield of chivalry that once existed in the guild of knights that was built upon the function of combat rather than scholarship and teaching. Honor gave the knight feudal security and also freedom.

We can see this most vividly, I think, in the concept of academic tenure. Tenure is—or was—the bond of protection for individuals possessed of knightly honor who gave faithfully and fully their services to the academic community. One had to earn it through both service and demonstrated quality of mind and character. Commonly, tenure was acquired with the rank of either associate professor or full professor. And once acquired, tenure could not be taken away from the individual for any reason short of flagrant, and fully demonstrated, debasing of academic mission. Rightly were codes of tenure cast in the most general of terms, invariably brief in statement, and without gratuitous detail of the specific kinds of offences that might result in withdrawal of tenure. Rightly was tenure guarded by the members of the guild of scholarly knights in the university. Rightly were many reasons found to justify, in the name of academic service, a privilege that was not enjoyed anywhere else in American society. For once examined carefully in terms of the criteria of individualism and democracy, the doctrine of tenure was a fragile one indeed.

Bear in mind that tenure was never extended by faculties to those other individuals—technicians, custodians, secretaries, even adminstrators or professional lawyers, physicians, and architects—working directly in salaried status for the university. For all of these something in the order of "job security" was deemed sufficient. But not tenure which, for professor as for medieval knight or monk, had roots in the notion of honor and of freedom that laity could not be expected to qualify for. I stress this. Tenure was never regarded by academics as properly belonging to any other professional or occupational group in society. Job security, yes, as with respect to the technicians and administrators working for universities. But not tenure. There was a quality to the concept of tenure and to the closely joined concept of academic freedom that can only be epitomized in the word *mystique*.

Academic freedom has or had the same aristocratic overtones that lie in tenure. I am not suggesting that professors believed that only they should possess freedom of mind and speech in society. That would be absurd. That a constitutionally based freedom should exist throughout society—for technicians, businessmen, workers, scholars, and citizens generally—was taken for granted by academic intellectuals. But the notion of freedom, as this existed in the traditional academic community, carried an additional, and much more specialized meaning. And this meaning was rooted deeply in the prior notion of the differential honor that inhered in scholarship and science. What this meaning suggested was that along with the ordinary civil and political rights possessed by all citizens in a democracy was the right flowing directly from academic function that made for full autonomy *in the performance of one's academic duties*. It was a right deemed as inhering in the role of professor in a given scholarly discipline in a way not to be found in any of the other roles in society. Only thus, it was argued, could the academic mission be fulfilled.

Recently the idea of academic freedom has become confused. We find it often invoked to justify a professor's nonacademic activities or beliefs in the surrounding social order. It is used, in short, as a kind of extra prop for the constitutional freedoms that he shares with other citizens. Students too have claimed academic freedom, utilizing the claim to emancipate their immoral, even their manifestly illegal, activities from scrutiny by the civil order. They have used it also, more compellingly, in support of their right to participate, along with professors, in the governing of the academic institution.

Without commenting here on the rightness or propriety of all such claims (and they may all be wholly justified), it is nonetheless important to emphasize that the historic concept of academic freedom was limited to faculties and to faculty members. It arose within the quasi-medieval structure that is the college or faculty today; it was nurtured by the communal properties of the structure; and, basically, it was inseparable from the special roles which were the elements of the structure.

When the doctrine received its first distinctive modern phrasing in early nineteenth-century Germany, it could be seen—just as could the pope's claim of infallibilty in matters of faith and morals—as a claim of immunity as well as a kind of compromise with the advancing forces of nationalism and mass democracy. What the pope said, in effect, was: with the loss of my temporal power, I nonetheless retain my absolute moral and spiritual power. What the German professors said, in effect, was: the university can no longer be the privileged enclave it has been since the Middle Ages; but even though the power of ultimate direction of finance has been taken over by the governmental ministry, we, the professors, reaffirm our historic right to autonomy in academic matters; that is, in matters other than financial, administrative, political, and so on. Which, obviously, meant largely the realm of teaching and of scholarship. As the pope affirmed his retention of a part of his former medieval liberty, so did the German professors affirm their retention of a part of what had been their medieval liberty.

But the German professors are distinguished only by the articulateness and explicitness of their affirmation. In one degree or other, the doctrine of academic freedom can be seen in all Western countries—nowhere more solidly than in Great Britain where it has had, until very recently, a scope and intensity often lacking in other countries, and this despite absence of very many pointed declarations in its behalf. Apart from a clear sense of both the tenure and the freedom that must inhere in any quasi-aristocratic organization, the American college and university would have found the going very rough indeed.

For, under that peculiarly American adaptation known as the lay board of trustees, and under the yoke that all too often sprang directly from Protestant auspices of American institutions, the danger of interference with both academic freedom and academic tenure was frequently an actual, not a merely potential, one. Respect for aristocratic privilege was not as great in the United States as it was among even the common people of Europe. The professor did not at any time in the nineteenth century enjoy the high status that his counterpart in Europe possessed almost as a matter of birthright. Salaries were low, status was relatively low, and the political influence of the university tended to be rather feeble until early in the present century. To a very large extent, it was with the European model, especially German, in mind that such stalwarts as John Dewey, Charles A. Beard, Arthur Lovejoy, and others active in the founding of the American Association of University Professors began just after World War I to drive home hard to the American people the indispensability to the university of both academic freedom and tenure. Constitutionally guaranteed freedoms and rights were not enough, as these wise men realized, to maintain the university in the manner of its European analogues.

It is important again to stress that when Dewey and Lovejoy declared boldly for academic freedom and tenure, they had in mind *only* professors, only those, in short, who formed the heart of the academic community and whose relation to what I have called the academic dogma was both clear and direct. Academic freedom meant to these scholars who founded the wider guild of professors in the United States freedom for *academic* man: not freedom for political man, economic man, or for those who believed the university to be primarily a privileged sanctuary for each and every dereliction, delinquency, and desolation of intellect known since Adam.

We must now turn to the changes in the American university which have led to destruction of not only academic freedom and tenure but also of the academic community of which these values are but necessary attributes.

PART II

The Degradation of
the Academic Dogma

5

THE HIGHER CAPITALISM

> The first man who, having enclosed a piece of ground, bethought himself of saying *This is mine,* and found people simple enough to believe him, was the real founder of civil society. From how many crimes, war, and murders, from how many horrors and misfortunes might not anyone have saved mankind, by pulling up the stakes, or filling up the ditch, and crying to his fellows, "Beware of this impostor; you are undone if you once forget that the fruits of the earth belong to us all, and the earth itself to nobody"
>
> ROUSSEAU, *A Discourse on the Origin of Inequality*

LET US PARAPHRASE. The first man who, having enclosed a piece of the university, bethought himself of saying, "This is my institute," and found members of the faculty simple enough to believe him, was the real founder of the university's higher capitalism. From how many corruptions, internecine wars, and bankruptcies might not any professor have saved the university by pulling up the stakes, by filling up the ditch, and crying to his fellow professors, "Beware of

71

this impostor; you are undone if you once forget that the fruits of the university belong to us all, and the university to nobody."

I can say it more simply. The first million dollars given to a university for project research was far too much. Today ten billion dollars is not enough. So have we fallen.

Beginning in the 1940s an immense amount of money began to flow into the more distinguished American universities: the universities whose style of living set the standard for all the rest. The dollar volume would be difficult to state exactly. Without any question, taking all spheres and aspects into view, many billions have been involved. If the physical sciences were the first to enjoy the new affluence, the social sciences and last of all, the humanities came to know such affluence in time. From federal government primarily but also state governments and, of course, foundations such as Ford huge sums began to pour into universities for the express purpose of research. *Project research.* It was all very much like the impact of gold bullion on the social structure of Western Europe in the sixteenth century. Not the *amount* of wealth. Rather, the *structure* of the wealth and the means by which the wealth transferred itself to members differentially in the community. The European community in the sixteenth century; the university community in the 1940s and the 1950s.

I firmly believe that direct grants from government and foundation to individual members of university faculties, or to small company-like groups of faculty members, for the purposes of creating institutes, centers, bureaus, and other essentially capitalistic enterprises within the academic community to be the single most powerful agent of change that we can find in the university's long history. For the first time in Western history, professors and scholars were thrust into the unwonted position of entrepreneurs in incessant search for new sources of capital, of new revenue, and, taking the word in its larger sense, of profits. Whereas for centuries the forces of commerce, trade, and industrialization outside the university had registered little if any impact upon the academic community beyond perhaps a certain tightening of forces within, the new capitalism, *academic capitalism,* is a force that arose within the university and that has had as its most eager supporters the members of the professoriat.

I am not suggesting that there is, or should be, any natural disaffinity between the university and wealth. Much less do I imply that members of the academic community should take vows of poverty anymore than of celibacy. There is no reason why the academic aristocracy should not be, in the good society, as wealthy as any landed aristocracy. That the professoriat has become, on the whole, somewhat more affluent during the past two or three decades, with at least some of its members men of substantial wealth and income by any standard, has nothing to do with what I am here concerned with. Had all academic salaries in the United States been trebled or quadrupled in the period right after the war—and I mean real salaries, real income—there is not the slightest reason for supposing that any significant change would have taken place in the nature of the university or in the character of academic roles. In earlier centuries, whether landed income for the aristocracy was very high in a given period, or very low, did not appreciably affect the character of the landed aristocracy. What was eventually to affect it was the impact of new opportunities for wealth which by their very nature struck at the heart of the structure of the aristocracy and at the nexus between aristocracy and society.

So too in the American university between about 1945 and 1965. New wealth, approaching billions, began to pour into universities from federal government, from industries, and from foundations. Had this wealth gone simply *to the universities,* somewhat after the fashion of governmental grants to the universities under the University Grants Commission in Great Britain, it is unlikely, it seems to me, that structural change in the university would have resulted or that major alterations in academic role, in academic authority, and in academic function would have occurred. Although the sums have been vast, they would no doubt have been assimilated through normal channels in ways that might have enriched but not, I think, transformed the academic community. Departments, faculties, schools, and colleges—these historic entities founded upon the fusion of teaching and scholarship —would not have suffered. Neither would the structure of allegiance and authority in the university, founded upon the roles of traditional academic committees, of department chairmen, of deans, provosts, and others. The age-old hierarchy, with the professors at the top and with the dean or president *primus inter pares,* would have undoubtedly survived as would have the old-age system of community and authority.

What in fact took place, as we know, was an assimilation of vast wealth through rather different channels. For the most part, traditional agencies in the university were bypassed, or given but token recognition, by government, industry, and foundation, with the new bullion going instead to academic entrepreneurs for companies known as centers, bureaus, and institutes. Overnight, first in the natural sciences, then in the social sciences, and finally—here and there, at least—in the humanities, the academic scene was bestridden by that modern incarnation of Caesar, the academic capitalist, the professorial entrepreneur, the new man of power!

The results have been fascinating to behold from the viewpoint of any sociologist of stratification, structure, or authority. At first the cloud on the horizon was no bigger than a man's hand. It was not easy—not at first—for the new wealth to diminish the hoary prestige of the guildsmen and aristocrats in the traditional university. But money in large amounts will not long be resisted. And to anyone in the late 1940s endowed with the kind of vision that might have come from reading either Tocqueville or Max Weber, it was clear that the small cloud on the horizon would become ever larger, reaching in time proportions capable of tempestuous effects in the universities. For the structure and the thrust of the new wealth that began pouring into the traditional university was simply incompatible, from the very beginning, with the latter's rather quaint system of authority.

A new breed of academic man was being formed; one that would soon have scant patience for the built-in checks and balances of the university, for the time-consuming systems of review by faculty committees, and for the stratified permissions of levels of administrators. Why should a chemist or biologist or—in due time—a sociologist or economist defer to faculty committee or dean, much less department chairman, when on his individual prestige alone hundreds of thousands of dollars, even millions, could be brought for use by retinues of technicians, graduate students, secretaries, and junior faculty members that would often rival established departments in size. Traditionally, much of the dean's or the research committee's prestige and authority had come from the fact that either might have a few thousands of dollars a year to allocate to worthy individuals for their research. Now, through individual entrepreneurship under the new capitalism, it was possible for almost any astute academic to get his hands on hundreds of thousands of dollars, occasionally even millions, and to do this without regard to the structure of authority in the university. This whole structure, which had once been a help to faculty members, now became in large measure a hindrance. A system of intermediate authority that had been designed, so to speak, to protect academic man from the market place, now seemed to many enterprising research titans an unwarranted invasion of their right to get to the market place.

Money, as Georg Simmel documented in his great study, has the power to effect change in society only when it penetrates social roles and social groups or when it becomes, in some novel way, the basis of new groups and roles. The vast sums that poured into the American university beginning about 1946 had both of these effects. Traditional, rather simple-minded, systems of accounting, or purchasing, of management generally, were of a sudden swamped by the sheer volume of the new wealth. Overnight a whole sector of administration, that concerned with finances and their proper handling, assumed unwonted importance in the academic-administrative hierarchy. The business and the managerial mind became increasingly vital. More and more, one observed a certain phenomenon, one strange to university ways. Men were now being chosen for chairmanships, deanships, and presidencies not because they were necessarily among the

light and leading of the academic community but because they
had something called "administrative" ability. And this ability
turned out to be not so much a skill or sensitivity to curricular problems but rather to problems of finance, production,
marketing, and especially salesmanship.

If the new capitalism in the American university had
altered only the administrative structure of the university, the
change would not have been really substantial. But just as
the capitalism of the seventeenth and eighteenth centuries in
Western Europe began early to affect the timeworn roles of
guildsmen, aristocrats, and tillers of the soil, so did the
academic capitalism of the 1940s and 1950s affect the roles
of professors and students, especially, at first, graduate students. The acids of the new finance could not help but eat
into the fabric of the traditional academic community.

And the cardinal reason for this impact upon the community was, as I have suggested, that the vast new wealth
emanating from government and foundation had as its goal not
the corporate university but the new academic entrepreneur,
who would manage it, use it, draw from it in novel ways.
The institute or center or bureau became the characteristic
agency of the new money just as the chartered company had
during Elizabethan days in England. All of a sudden the
academic landscape was the scene of literally hundreds of
such organizations coming into being, from Berkeley to Harvard. Sometimes they were entirely separate in their appointments. Other times a kind of joint appointive relation existed
between institute and academic department. But the difference here was not very important, for in either instance the
center of gravity was to be found in the institute or center,
not the traditional department.

No doubt the impact of the new capitalism on the American university would have been much less if these institutes and centers had been designed more or less after the model of those of nineteenth- and early twentieth-century Europe. For there the institute combined the functions of teaching with research. The function of the European institute indeed was the time-honored academic function, arising directly from what I have called the academic dogma, of inducting novitiates into the scholarship of some reigning academic figure. A great many American scholars and scientists received their crucial instruction as graduate students in these European institutes at the turn of the present century. If the European institute tended to be built in the first instance around research, most notably in Germany, its function nonetheless extended clearly and creatively into the realm of teaching.

In the American university, however, the kind of institute that came so richly into being after World War II was limited by prescription as well as scholarly preference substantially to research alone. After all, it was the function of the *department* to teach. In the institute or center, *research* would be done. And although the genius of the traditional department in the American university had lain in its fusion of research and teaching, a gulf now began to be apparent between the two, with inevitable status implications. More and more, one became aware of "department-oriented" individuals on the campus and of "institute-oriented" members of the faculty. Increasingly, the first came to be thought of as locals and the second as cosmopolitans. And whereas for generations university and college campuses in this country had existed without this distinction being drawn, now, all of a sudden, it became a vital one. Once again in history wealth, that is, new wealth, had proved its capacity for dislocating status structure in a social order.

The final point I want to make about the economic aspect of the Great Transformation, before turning to the political consequences in the university, is related to the sheer size of research grants. I do not see how one can conclude other than that size of grant makes a kind of quantum difference. A small grant is often reconcilable with undiminished teaching and performance of other obligations in the academic community. Research develops with teaching just as teaching develops with research. But this is true only so long as the context of the former is small enough to permit—nay, to demand—the participation of the student, in one or other degree. It is true only so long, in short, as the central figure remains, *can* remain, an integral part of the academic community.

In many ways the most notable aspect of the period that began after the war—that began with the war in the physical sciences—is the sheer magnitude of university-accepted research responsibility. One began to be conscious of single institutes exceeding in the volume of their research production entire campuses before the war. Research of a scale, and also of a type, that had before been left to the great industrial laboratories or to federal or state departments, was now being eagerly taken on by universities and their institutes. The granting agencies preferred to deal in large sums, and such was the prestige of large sums of money among the academic *nouveaux riches* that large sums were sought, even though a veritable transformation in the lives of the holders of institute memberships was involved. Whereas small research of a type done even by the Ernest Lawrences, Gilbert Lewises, and

Herbert McLean Evanses at Berkeley in the sciences prior to World War II was easily combined with an undiminished luster of the academic department, as well as with teaching and with membership in the community, the new, vast, highly organized and bureaucratized research was not. Nor could it have been.

Theoretically, at least, there was a choice possible in the American university down until about 1950. We might have turned our backs on the new wealth with its built-in demands for a radical restructuring of the university and said, in effect: we shall continue with research of a degree of size, individuality, and character that the university has always known; a type of research that is reconcilable with the sovereign role of teaching in the university; of teaching-in-scholarship, of scholarship-in-teaching. This type of research, we might have said, is the type reflected in the seminal works of such scientists as Bridgman at Harvard, Fermi in Rome, Lewis at Berkeley, Morgan at Caltech, and so on. Small in scope, its hallmark is its easy flexibility, its spontaneity, its freedom from the managerial demands of large-scale organizations. And it not only can be fused with the responsibilities of teaching; but by its nature it has to be. This is the university's proper definition of research. Other types of research, the kind known as "development," the kind that by its nature must be huge in size, calling for large managerial staffs, complete with workers and technicians, we choose to leave to government and to large industry.

We might have said this. But we didn't. And I suppose on reflection it would have been astonishing if we had. When in history have aristocracies turned their backs on substantial amounts of money, no matter what the source or probable

long-run social effect? Certainly, there were few landed aristocrats in the British eighteenth and nineteenth centuries who
turned their backs on commerce, industry, and the other
sources of great new wealth. Why should we today expect
academic aristocrats of the 1940s to have turned their backs
on the vast sums of money which in the federal government,
the big foundations, and large industry, in effect, lay waiting
for the magic word. The magic word was, of course, *project.*
And it was the project system that converted scholars into
managers of research enterprises—with *research,* as a word,
gradually succeeding scholarship in prestige. It was difficult,
after all, to make effective use of the word "scholarship" in
some of the new enterprises in the forms of institute, center,
and bureau that were flooding American campuses by the
1950s.

"Things and actions," wrote Bishop Butler, "are what they
are, and the consequences of them will be what they will be;
why, then, should we desire to be deceived?" Putting the
present matter a little differently, why should we desire to
be deceived about the nature and the consequences of the
project system? It is always fashionable in universities and
colleges to blame industry, profession, and government for
all the ills that befall academic man. Even now a mythology
is forming that makes big government and big industry responsible for the degradation of the academic dogma, for the
conversion of scholarship into organized, factory-like research,
for the transformation of literally thousands of professors from
teachers and scholars into entrepreneurs of the research dollar, business and government consultants, managers, directors
of essentially industrial organizations on the campus, and,
most recently, founders of lucrative businesses just far enough

outside academic walls to escape university patent regulations.

But all of this, the mythology notwithstanding, is the direct result of *academic* choice: or, putting it concretely, of individual choices by large numbers of faculty members in the period following the war for this selfsame conversion and transformation. Today, at every hand, students and faculty members on the left decry that tiny part of the project system that involves "secret" research for federal, chiefly defense, agencies. But this is like decrying the pustule in a smallpox epidemic and giving no thought to the larger contexts. One thing is very clear: there would be no vast laboratories, institutes, and centers on the American campus today, doing business with Pentagon or CIA, had the fateful decision not been made in the 1940s *to do business.*

I have personally talked with a half-dozen major executive figures in American industry, representing corporations that have let out, so to speak, their work to academics. No one could have been more surprised than these corporation figures at the eagerness, the rapacity, with which scientists—social and physical—seized at the waiting money. I venture the guess that there was more lament among university and college alumni in the business world than there was on the campus when the transformation of the American university commenced a quarter-century ago, with the degradation of the academic dogma the clear result. It was not only lament; there was rich disillusionment. "Scratch a faculty member today," observed one industrial vice-president," and you almost always find a businessman." My acquaintance sounded a little sad as he said it.

It will perhaps be said that the project system on the campus was not really capitalism or commercialism inasmuch as personal profit was not usually the motivation of the professor. But Berle and Means taught us in their classic *Modern Corporation and Private Property* that personal profit is rarely if ever the chief motivation of the corporation titan in the modern world of business. It is not to the supposed profit motive of Adam Smith's corner tradesman that we must look, declared the authors of this book, when we seek the springs of modern business. We would do better to look to the motivations of a Napoleon or a Bismarck. In such motivations are to be found, compounded, desires for status and power, as well as financial gain alone. And, as Schumpeter pointed out in his *Capitalism, Socialism, and Democracy,* even the nineteenth-century individual businessman obeyed, not individual lust for gain but, rather, lust for gain for his family or his company. So with the research titan who began in the late 1940s to govern the American university campus.

Suffice it to say that the Chaucerian scholar whom I have earlier used in these pages as something of a protagonist, an archetype, in the academic community no longer walked so tall on the campus. He and his fellows in the humanities, the social sciences, and even the physical sciences, who continued to regard the proper work of the university as that of teaching and individual scholarship, who thought that industry is the place for industrialism, government the place for military research, labor organizations the place for labor-relations consulting, were, by the end of the 1950s, towered over by those who, in the glow of the new capitalism, felt very differently on these matters.

As I say, many of us will go on indefinitely blaming business, government, and foundation for the degradation of the academic dogma. Students and faculty alike will continue to blame our difficulties on "bad" large-scale research, such as that done for Pentagon, exonerating completely the academic capitalism that arises from the vast sums of money coming from the multitudinous nonmilitary agencies in society. Even the military is coming in for a special academic-liberal dispensation nowadays, however. This springs from the large sums of money going from the military to, not only physicists, chemists, and biologists, but also to social scientists (humanists tomorrow?) for what is solemnly called basic research. Basic research, the academic litany goes, has a transfiguring, a cleansing effect on the granter, no matter how military his identity, provided only that it is really basic research.

Already the lesson of Project Camelot is being forgot by academics in the glow of academic capitalism. In this project, which I have described at length elsewhere,[1] a considerable number of American social scientists were so bemused by the offer of six million dollars, for purposes of investigating the causes of radicalism and revolt, that they allowed themselves to forget not only the identity of the granter—the United States Army—but the fact that the study was to be conducted, more or less confidentially, in other nations: nations, as it turned out to the surprise of no freshman student in elementary sociology or political science, that did not relish such "research."

Project Camelot blew up in the faces of its creators. It never involved, at any time during its brief existence, more than a handful of social scientists. Still, once the full details of this project were brought, by congressional inquiry, for all

[1] See my "Project Camelot: An Autopsy," *The Public Interest* (Fall 1966), reprinted in my *Tradition and Revolt* (New York: Random House, Vintage Book, 1970).

to see, there were large numbers of academics, in all spheres, who must have said to themselves: there but for the grace of God go I.

Most of the sense of embarrassment, even of guilt, that seized many members of the scientific establishment immediately following exposure of Project Camelot has long since vanished. The roots of what I have called academic capitalism are far too deep for anything like this minor scandal to leave serious effect. And, as we know, these roots become ever deeper, their foliage and bloom ever more dense on the American campus.

It would not do to end this chapter on the higher capitalism of the late 1940s and the 1950s without noting, however briefly, the general affluence that spread rapidly through university channels in those years. Something comparable to a quantum jump took place in the university's standard of living in all spheres. Given the very substantial dollar overrides to the university administration that went with all of these entrepreneurial projects (rarely less than 25 percent, often greater, I am told), it is not strange that both the administration itself and also the whole network of activities and things controlled by administration—design and luxury of buildings, parks, roads, walkways, salaries, and perquisites of all kinds—should have participated in the incidental benefits of the new wealth.

Everywhere a sudden rise in affluence and luxury could be seen taking place. Had it been confined solely to those things that were central to the university—teaching and scholarship —it is doubtful that this rise would have had much general effect. Teachers and scholars in the university are, or certainly were, by nature rather impervious to the charms of these manifestations of wealth. (As I have repeatedly said, they were, within academic walls at least, an aristocracy, with aristocracy's common dislike of ostentation.) But the sharp increase in affluence was to be seen everywhere. Buildings suddenly became luxurious, as did campus landscapes. Dormitories not seldom resembled luxury hotels. A veritable faculty jet set came into being, to excite envy—and emulation. The ways in which the new wealth of the higher capitalism showed are too numerous for mention. And had anyone objected at the time, he would surely have been put down as a reactionary, as one too selfish, too undemocratic, too antediluvian to appreciate the right to all good things that professors and students, and all others in the university, are entitled to.

And if anyone did ask from the outside, as Irving Kristol did in a now historic article on the financing of universities, whether the combined wealth of foundation and government would be sufficient in the future to maintain the university in the luxurious style to which it was becoming accustomed, he could be overlooked on the ground that while his arguments were not answerable, "continuing economic growth" and inevitable progress would take care of everything. Trustees, themselves businessmen, university administrators, the project titans, faculty members in all spheres, students, and even the general public became accustomed to, became actually dependent on, the spectacle of the higher capitalism on the American campus and of all its attributes of affluence and privilege.

The spirit of entrepreneurship began in the physical and biological sciences. It widened steadily and at rising speed in the social sciences in the postwar period. Even the humanities

and fine arts were not, however, very far behind. The entrepreneurial spirit could be seen in the drama department, the
art department, the music department, but also, increasingly,
in the hoary departments of history, literature, and philosophy. Nothing on earth is more contagious than affluence. And
few things more corrupting can be found on earth—especially
in those areas of function that are by their nature utterly un-
prepared to deal with it.

⚗ 6 ⚗

THE NEW MEN OF POWER

By THE EARLY 1950s a new type of individual was everywhere to be seen rising to mastery on the American campus. It is not easy to describe him. He resembled neither the traditional professor nor the traditional administrator on the campus. Not likely by either substance or manner to be mistaken for the scholar, he was nevertheless invariably associated with research: Big Research. Teaching did not often interest him. Nor did the simple chores and requirements of the academic department. For that matter he was not interested in administration, at least in the traditional sense of a deanship, a provostship, much less a department chairmanship. None of these commanded the prestige and sheer wealth that went with positions on the campus of a very different kind: the directorships of the fast-multiplying institutes, centers, and bureaus which were the contexts of the higher capitalism.

What I now want to do is describe this new breed in its political rather than economic role. And well I might. For the political impact of the new breed, these new men of power, was, of all influences upon the traditional academic community, the most direct, in the long run the most shattering.

To be sure this new creature was not without prototype. There were institutes and directors before World War II. But they were few and rarely of any consequence. Nor were their prestige, status, or influence of any notable significance —not, certainly, by comparison with that of a provost, dean, or even a department chairman. For in the areas presided over by these traditional figures—areas without exception of *combined teaching and research*—lay all the real action. Even, as I shall stress in some detail below, where full-time research organizations were present in the university, as in the agricultural institutes and field stations (limited for the most part to the Land Grant universities), they were always kept distant from the flow of regular activities of the university and, by far most importantly, were thoroughly subordinated to the academic centers of influence and authority. The essential point, though, is that institutes and centers were extremely few in number and in no case ever rivaled in importance the departments, schools, and colleges in the university, each of which was, by its very nature, built around the teaching function. And certainly the institute member did not rival the professor!

The higher capitalism changed all this in the years immediately following World War II. Not only, as a result of the vast influx of new wealth, specifically marked for research institutes, did their numbers increase almost exponentially, but their political influence within the university also shot up immediately with predictably dire consequences to the older centers of authority.

The new men of power, representing as they did great wealth gained through their own acumen, were not likely to share this power with the traditional councils and committees and administrators. In precisely the same way that the new men of power of the Renaissance and Enlightenment—lawyers, advisers to monarchs, administrators—took pains to by-pass the old, medieval-in-origin parlements and councils of Europe, the better to strengthen both state and economy, as it was believed, so did our new men of academic power in the late 1940s and the 1950s. Increasingly, as one looks back on the situation in this country, from Berkeley to Harvard, one sees that while token gestures were indeed made to faculties and faculty committees, the thrust was in the direction of direct power: power gained directly from trustees and presidents.

These latter, dazzled by the research reputations of some of the institute directors, already committed to the "star" system that, during the decade of the 1950s, was to make the search for established name and talent as competitive as anything to be found in professional football or baseball (but, alas, without the reserve clause in the academic world), were for the most part willing to do anything that would hold their institute and bureau "stars" on the campus. And anyhow who in his right mind among the trustees would do anything to cut off the funds the new men of power were bringing to their enterprises in the university?

Hence the momentous shift in power that began to take place on the American university campus in the decade after the war and, with it, the always crucial shift in the center, the effective center, of allegiance of faculty members. For a very ingenious system came into being; one known as the "joint appointment" in which a given individual would hold appointment part-time in an academic department and part-time in an institute, usually on a fifty-fifty basis, with salary source divided accordingly. The intent, or at least rationalization, of the joint appointment system was exemplary: rather than have, it was said, usually rather piously, any likelihood of independent institutes, which might distract from the academic character of both institute and university, let us instead make certain that institute and university are closely joined. Let us prevent the rise of disruptive allegiances among faculty members that would surely be the consequence of institutes and projects whose principal figures were appointed solely to these enterprises. Let us have in our institutes only those who are at the same time members of academic, that is, *teaching,* departments.

A shrewder way of guaranteeing the permanence of the institute or project on the campus could scarcely have been devised. And, from the strict sociological point of view, a shrewder way of in fact diminishing the real authority and influence of the older academic divisions of the university, colleges, schools, and departments, could scarcely have been devised. Men's allegiances and devotions are prone to go to the functions and authorities in society that carry the greatest status appeal, not to mention ready wealth. One may indeed be, in theory, half-time in a teaching department and half-time in an institute. But the evidence began to be very clear indeed by 1950 that the "halftime" in the department usually meant a single course a term and an hour or two of so-called counselling. To the institute, if the faculty member was so fortunate as to belong to one, went the rest of his time and, given the accelerating drive toward big research with its troops of student-technicians earning a handsome living, went a substantial part of the graduate student population. Certainly, to the institute went the overwhelming part of the faculty member's real devotion, real allegiance. It soon ceased to matter what department you were in; what mattered was your institute or center. And, for all the obvious reasons, the power of the institute, the center, and the project, expressed through directors and their principal academic figures, increased constantly.

Rarely was any of this crude. Generally it was scarcely evident at the time of the crucial transfer of power. Ancient academic rituals continued, with the manner, if not always the substance, of deference before academic committees and academic chairmen and deans. If one was an astute director —and one usually was!—he did not make the mistake of offending needlessly. Always he asked even when he and the committee or the dean being asked both knew that the asking was supererogatory. After all, the great Augustus in the first century, even after he had become Princeps for Rome, always scrupulously asked the Senate for permission. And it was only when Augustus's lineal successor Caligula appointed his favorite horse to the Senate that reality suddenly burst into the obvious. So with the university in the 1950s. Traditional orders of precedence continued in the commencement march; traditional orders of precedence also continued in the agenda of faculty meetings. There was, in short, nothing crude, nothing offensive, about the rise to effective power of the new breed, the new men of power in the university. And, as I have said, the genius of the joint-appointment system was such that the institutes and centers could capture the allegiances of faculty members under the marvelous fiction that it was allegiance to department that was really being strengthened.

In the 1960s, when student militants challenged the authority of the faculty, the departments, colleges, and schools —chiefly, as we know, in the humanities and social sciences —they could have reminded the committees and administrators they were so calculatedly humiliating that the first challenge to academic authority had come from the prestige-laden directors and titans of the postwar capitalistic enterprises on the campus. And they would have been right. For, above any other single influence in the eroding of academic authority and its base, the academic community, the force of the institute, project, and center principals stand supreme. By the time the student militants hurled their defiances at the authority of the faculty and the traditional administration, there was very little authority left that could be mustered. There was really nothing to do but call the police. I shall come back to this in more detail in a later chapter. But it would be wrong to omit it here from discussion.

I can think of no better way of illustrating and also emphasizing the shift of power that took place in the 1950s than by use of the academic department as an example. Just as I used the Chaucerian scholar in an early chapter as the personification of authority and influence of the traditional academic dogma, I will now use the figure of the traditional department chairman.

It will no doubt come as a surprise, even a shock, to younger members of the faculty today, as well as to students, to realize that down until about 1950 the post of department chairman was one of the most widely honored, and also deeply coveted, positions on the American university campus.

Rare indeed was the teacher-scholar, however great his renown, who did not feel it incumbent on loyalty and honor to career to accept a department chairmanship when it was proffered.

Considered as an *administrative* post, the chairmanship was as high as one could go in the university without giving one's full time to administration, without sacrificing teaching and scholarly interests. The chairman was expected to maintain his academic vigor and, with rarest exceptions, he did. There was little difficulty, prior to the advent of the administrative problems which beset American universities from 1945 on, in combining the relatively light duties of the chairman's office with continuing work in classroom, laboratory, or study. And considered as an *academic* post—which it was—it was everywhere regarded as the highest possible recognition that one's colleagues and the administration could bestow upon a teacher-scholar.

The esteem which went with the chairmanship was grounded in the significance of the department in the American university. The department was, so to speak, the university *in parvo*. It was the effective, the operating, context of the two great functions of the university: teaching and scholarship. It was the academic man's strongest loyalty within his university, the source of much of whatever prestige he may have borne, and the chief repository of academic authority. Scholarship, curriculum, teaching, service to society, all of these converged in the academic department. The department was in the American university substantially what the "faculty" was in the European universities.

It would be absurd to pretend that the department was in all respects ideal. The present, largely pejorative implication of the word "departmental" arises in considerable part from the sectarian jealousies that could exist among departments, from the all too common effort of departments to capture the curricular time of their students. More than a few otherwise distinguished minds lost sight of the heights of Olympus because of the puny breastworks sometimes set up by departments. None of this is to be doubted.

But the department was nonetheless a very useful way of combining into one unit the dual function of the university professor: teaching and research. Moreover, by its nature, the department did not have to depend upon the always fragile, generally ephemeral, zeal or *enthusiasm* (in the eighteenth-century religious sense of that word) for its operation year after year, decade after decade, that is obliged to go into so many of the nondepartmental, "experimental" programs that have proliferated during the last few years. In these latter, structure usually collapses with the waning of zeal, the spending of passion. Not so the department.

Good or bad, however, the department was without any question the central unit of the American university prior to the advent of centers, institutes, and bureaus in their large numbers. The prestige that today goes only with the role of research-institute director went then with the role of department chairman. More important, there was substantial opportunity for personal leadership, for the use of imagination and of influence in the building of a great department, in the making of crucial appointments, in the setting of policy, in the formation of curriculum. Beyond the department itself, the chairman's voice was bound to be influential in the higher councils that advised deans and presidents. Who else was there to give this advice, to wield this campus-wide influence, prior to about 1945? Institute and center directors had not yet entered the scene, save in negligible numbers. Faculty and administrative committees had not yet become the powerful means of bypassing the department they were to become by 1950.

Granted that, in the better universities at least, the chairman was obliged to consult his colleagues—senior colleagues —on important matters, and that his choice of new faculty members was always limited, at least in theory, by final approval of the dean or president. The fact remains, the chairman was a powerful figure. And, as the histories of distinguished American departments make clear, the chairman was a crucial figure. No wonder then, strange as it may seem today, that great scholars in great universities could hope for, look forward to, even plot and scheme for, the chairman's position. And this was true across the country, from Harvard to Berkeley.

It no longer is true, of course. The substantially altered position of the department in the American university authority-system has seen to that. For the blunt fact is, the academic department carries today very little of the functional importance it once did. Its luster has been dimmed by the luster of the institute and the center. It surely has not escaped attention from anyone in the university that whereas the distinguished scholar will today jump at the opportunity to become a director of his own research organization on the campus, he is likely to regard with distaste, even repugnance, the duties of chairman of a department. How often indeed have not acceptances of appointments to senior professorships stipulated that under no circumstances will service as chairman be expected?

No doubt there are circumstances in which this diminished role of the department, and of the department chairman, could be salutary. There is nothing sacrosanct about the department or any other single academic-administrative unit. The difficulty is that *nothing has really replaced the department as a genuinely significant unit of combined teaching and research.* The institutes which have proliferated on the campus are overwhelmingly—despite the research fellowships they usually embody for graduate students and for those in postdoctoral status—concerned with research alone. Teaching has become, in effect, the function of the department. This too would be perhaps salutary if it were not for the conspicuous degradation of the teaching function that is itself, I believe, an aspect of the degradation of the department. Academic men are no longer dependent upon the department to the degree they once were. Nor are they dependent, as they once were, upon the teaching function.

I do not want to exaggerate the significance of the department and of the department chairmanship. I have used each as a telling illustration of the kind of decline of authority that can take place under the impact of new and more effective authorities. What is really important is not the department alone but the larger structure of authority that once existed in the university, itself the product of the universally conceived function of the university in society: the indirect service to society that flowed directly from the academic dogma with its twin responsibilities of acquiring knowledge and of disseminating it in classroom and seminar.

Not in department alone but also in those collections of departments, or department members, we call faculties rested a fair share of the weight of academic authority. So too did it rest on certain academic councils and committees. One and all these faculties, councils, and committees were concerned, not with teaching alone, nor with research alone, but with *combined* teaching and research. The atom of the academic role had not yet become split. Admittedly, there were, under the old system, bad teachers as there were bad scholars. No system can generate great teaching or scholarship out of turnips. And in the past as in the present, the American university has its full due of these. But they do not affect the matter, which is one of the nature of the university's mission and the locus of its authority over courses, curricula, faculty appointments, students, and members of the faculty themselves.

Suffice it to say that, beginning just after World War II, the locus of authority in the university was, and continues to be, profoundly muddled, fragmented, atomized, as the case may be. What I have illustrated by the dislocation of the department from academic centrality could as easily be illustrated by reference to any one of the many contexts of authority—academic, administrative, and academic-administrative—that were themselves reflections of the university's mission in society. And the chief cause of this disintegration of academic authority is precisely that vast new wealth which underlay what I have called the new capitalism and which obtruded itself in the forms of projects and institutes.

Just as these projects and institutes were centers of wealth, so were they centers of authority. By their nature they conflicted, had to conflict, with the traditional sources of authority in the university. The first real revolt against academic authority was not that of the students but of faculty members. I refer, of course, to those faculty members who by their own prowess managed to draw large sums of money from government or foundation and who, as enterprisers generally do, insisted upon the immunity of their projects, centers, and institutes from the authority of either department or of corporate faculty. Whereas there had been, for the most part, an unbroken chain of authority in the university, with department, faculty, and college or school its links—each of these a unit of teaching and research—there now existed on most American university campuse a plethora of new structures that did not, and generally would not, become links in this chain of traditional authority. To use an old term of jurisprudence, the institute became an *imperium in imperio*.

This, then, marks the second major aspect of the degradation of the academic dogma: the decline in the historically evolved structure of authority that flowed through all aspects of academic life, touching faculty members as well as students. Very much as commercial and manufacturing companies arose some centuries ago in the interstices of the guild system, of traditional society generally, so did the great and powerful new projects and institutes arise, beginning a quarter of a century ago, outside, or in the interstices, of traditional academic authority.

No one who was on the American university campus when the large research institutes began to flourish is likely to forget the shifts which took place in authority, in influence, in wealth, and in status. Overnight, it seemed, two nations came into being: the haves and the have-nots; the first possessed of a form of wealth and power that owed little if anything to the university; the second identified increasingly by their lack of research money, their dependence upon the university, their largely local identities, and then ever-diminishing status in the eyes of not only administration and faculty but, in due time, of the students. For students know with unerring instinct where the power lies. The science of who gets what and how is an exact science in the contemporary university.

Thus, when the student militants began their onslaught against the university and its system of authority in the early 1960s, their work was made easy by the intellectual confusion, the transvaluation of values, and the sense of drift rather than mastery that were the inescapable consequences of an earlier onslaught—though, of course, a very subtle one— that the new capitalists, the new men of power, had already conducted a few years before. With the authority of the department, the faculty, the academic senate already diminished, there was really little to fear.

𝒲 7 𝒲

THE ACADEMIC BOURGEOISIE

T HE BOURGEOISIE," wrote Marx and Engels, "wherever it has got the upper hand, has put an end to all feudal, patriarchal, idyllic relations. It has pitilessly torn asunder the motley feudal ties that bound man to his 'natural superior,' and has left remaining no other nexus between man and man than naked self-interest, than callous 'cash payment.' It has drowned the most heavenly ecstasies of religious fervor, of chivalrous enthusiasm, of philistine sentimentalism, in the icy water of egotistical calculation." [1]

Allowing only for the tractarian cast of those words, they come fairly close to describing the change that could be seen taking place in the American university by the early 1950s. The new wealth from government bureaus and the foundations, the new structures for this wealth provided by dazzled trustees, administrators, and faculty in the forms of institutes, centers, and bureaus, and the whole entrepreneurial atmosphere that began to envelop the university could

[1] *The Communist Manifesto.*

not help but produce a new class on the American campus: a new bourgeoisie.

True, this class insisted upon retaining the earlier privileges of feudal estate all the while availing itself, through new roles and statuses, of the bullion that came pouring onto the campus. So, as a number of studies have shown, did the rising European businessman of the fifteenth and sixteenth centuries. It has doubtless always been this way in history. Feudal or patriarchal titles are best when they cover nonfeudal, nonpatriarchal types of wealth and power.

There are several ways of understanding the change that began to come over the campus in the 1950s as the result of the spread of the new academic bourgeoisie. One way is through the famous typology of Sir Henry Maine: from *status to contract.* More and more, relations on the campus began to resemble, not the timeworn ties of an academic knighthood, or patrimonial estate, or monastery, but rather the ties of an ordinary business establishment. From *member* of the university the faculty member passed to *employee.* Granted that even to this moment nothing outrages academic man as does some trustee's gauche reference to the faculty as "employees." As we have seen, it was an article of faith in the traditional academic community that whereas technicians and secretaries were employees, the faculty was not. Nevertheless, the change I speak of was brought on the university largely by the faculty itself: more especially by the higher capitalists and the new men of power on university faculties.

The transition I refer to was symbolized perfectly, it seems to me, when, starting around 1950 one began to hear the word "hire" more and more commonly around university halls. In earlier periods of university history, one did not *hire* a professor, as one did, say, a lawyer, engineer, or other professional. One *appointed* a professor to his institution. I suppose careful research would reveal that the same linguistic fate befell the feudal knight even before the spread of gunpowder when, with capitalistic policies becoming ever more attractive to kings and feudal lords, these latter commenced "hiring" knights rather than investing them with feudal responsibilities. In any event this fate befell the American professor in the early 1950s, and it can be said to mark one more degree to which the atmosphere of capitalism was fast replacing that of feudalism, to the highly evident satisfaction of all concerned. Department chairmen could be heard in rising volume describing their responsibility as that of "hiring staff," with the latter of these two words reflecting in its own way the degradation of professorial status, the subtle but puissant welding of faculty identity to that of the identities of others on the campus whose duties were technical or manual and whose relation to the university had always been of different quality or intensity.

Still another, and more substantial, way of noting the transition of the American university from community to corporation is in the terms of *professionalism*. This word must be defined very carefully here, however. I am not referring to the influence of the traditional professional schools on the campus. Despite the nonsense that has been written by lay preachers of the so-called liberal arts, the university was founded in the first place for professional purposes: for the training of theologians, lawyers, and physicians. It is as absurd today as it was in the 1930s when Robert M. Hutchins first began his fulminations against the

professional schools and departments to liken the "true
university" to a monastic seat of tranquil contemplation.
Training for professions is what the universities are all about.
Even at the old Oxford and Cambridge, where professional
schools did not exist as they did on the Continent and in the
United States, where the classics lasted longest as the essence
of a university degree, it was always assumed that, for the
brightest and ablest of minds at least, the purpose of the education was preparation for a profession—civil service,
clergy, or law.

It is a point to be emphasized and even reemphasized here
that the existing professional schools on American university
campuses in the period just after World War II had almost
nothing to do with the transformation, the degradation, of the
American university I am describing in this book. Such a
statement may come as a shock to those whose stock in trade
has been, ever since the rise of the cults of individuality and
of the liberal arts in the American university, to beat professional schools over their heads. But the evidence is very
clear on this point. With the fewest exceptions—engineering
leading among them perhaps—the professional schools resisted the virus of entrepreneurialism, of the higher capitalism,
to a degree not found, among departments of economics,
biology, mathematics, sociology, physics, and other bastions
of the traditional academic community.

The record of schools of law is especially clear in this
regard. Rare indeed during the two decades following the
war was the law school that took to itself the kind of institute
or project, the batteries of technicians and assistants, that one
found in rising intensity coming out of allegedly liberal arts
departments. To the present moment I dare say one is far

more likely to come upon individual teaching (complete with
reading of student examinations and frequent hours of consultation) and individual research in, say, the Harvard Law
School than in the Harvard departments of sociology, English,
and biology—much less physics and chemistry.

But my intent here is not to praise the professional schools,
most of which by this time have accumulated a large enough
burden of guilt in the degradation of the academic dogma. It
is rather to highlight the special kind of professionalism that
overtook the key departments of the academic community
during the 1950s.

The essence of the matter is this: whereas professionality
in the school of medicine or law in the traditional university
expressed itself in curriculum, in content of course, and in
clear professional objective for students graduating from the
professional school, in the new professionalism expressed itself in ways that tended to bypass, even flout, curriculum
and course. In the older professional schools—which were
few in any event on the American campus, despite the absurd
inflation of the matter by Robert Hutchins and his followers—
one pointed to what he taught and wrote as evidence of his
professionalism. In post-World War II departments of economics, biology, physics, and mathematics, on the other
hand, one pointed, for evidence of his recently acquired
professionality, not to content of course and curriculum but to
the innumerable consultantships, practices, jobs in industry
and government, and other forms of genteel moonlighting
that mushroomed in these and many other areas. Above all,
if one was in one or other of these once proudly aristocratic
areas of the academic community, he pointed to his project
or institute payroll, to his facility at getting grants, to the

dollar volume of the latest "job" assumed by his institute, and, of course, to his familiarity with the light and leading of the industrial, foundation, and bureaucratic worlds.

Say what one wishes about the evils of professionalism in the older schools, including their all too common descent from professionality to mere occupationalism. The fact remains that the greatest, or at least most notorious, feats of bourgeois grantsmanship during the period I am concerned with came out of departments of physics, biology, and sociology. As is too well known to bear slightest further mention here, it was not what your grant actually was aimed at doing; it was the dollar volume of the grant and the social status of the agency from which the grant came; *this* was what mattered, as it indeed still does.

For the vast majority of departments before World War II "profession" meant quite simply and exclusively the university itself. This is an important fact psychologically. As long as the university was one's profession—with identity as chemist or political scientist or mathematician secondary to this—one was bound to give it first devotion. Very different was the situation once one's profession as chemist, political scientist, and mathematician took priority.

Whereas, prior to the 1940s, the overwhelming majority of academic fields, in sciences as well as humanities, had disciplinary visibility chiefly within the academic community, all of these fields began—some earlier than others—to assume greater distinctiveness as professions, as combinations of study, teaching, and practice, and hence no longer dependent as they had once been upon Alma Mater. The beginnings of this transition can be seen in the 1940s. By the mid-1950s the transition had been wholly accomplished in the natural sciences, largely in the social sciences, and beginnings could be seen even within the humanities, where the roles of "writer," "poet," "critic," and "novelist" could be seen vying strenuously with the roles of professor and scholar.

Once, to be a physicist or sociologist meant beyond any possible question that one held academic rank in a college or university. Today each is much more like an engineer or a physician. To be a sociologist or political scientist today means that one is probably an academic man (more probably, on the evidence, than if one is a chemist or economist or psychologist), but he may easily be in government, in private industry, or even, with shingle out, in consulting practice. From being primarily and essentially a university member whose field was, more or less incidentally, sociology, one is today, increasingly, a sociologist whose job is, more or less incidentally, held within the university. No single transition within the past quarter-century has been more fateful, it seems to me, than this one. It could not help but change profoundly the historic relation of academic man to the university.

If, on the evidence, more and more academic men in the universities were taking increased satisfaction in their new roles of professionals—working for, but in no substantial way committed to the institution from which they might be drawing a part of their dollar income—administrators, trustees, and the lay public could be forgiven if they joined academic men themselves in references to the "hiring" of "staff," and if they began to substitute in their own minds the concept of "employee" for the hoary concept of faculty member, with its associations of a tie to the university that went beyond the nexus of cash.

I should stress here that there is no intrinsic reason whatever why professionalization of one's status should not have become the due of sociologists, economists, and even members of departments of literature whose prestige as novelists, poets, or literary essayists rivalled their prestige as teachers and scholars. There is inherently no reason why engineers, physicians, and lawyers should hold a visible professional status in addition to academic status that cannot be readily found for sociologists, psychologists, and economists. Who will doubt that fact in the burgeoning society of the twentieth century with its complex problems of government, business, finance, seeking to remain viable in these areas as in those of individual health and of physical technology. There is assuredly a needed place for the professional sociologist, economist, biologist, chemist, and mathematician, for the individual who takes his learning and skill to the wider society for direct application, just as does the physician and lawyer. None of this is in question here.

But it is worth repeating: the fundamental difference between the old and the new professionalism lay exactly in the contrasting attitudes toward curriculum, toward teaching, toward the academic community as the center of the intellectual universe, and toward the several criteria by which one assessed himself or was assessed by others. One could be a distinguished professor of law, in the old professionalism, and never leave campus, never seek a grant or directorship in foundation or on-campus institute, never hire a technician, never engage a teaching or research assistant, never even attend meetings of the American Bar Association. To think of trying to become a distinguished—let us say successful—professor of sociology or physics or biology during the period 1945–1960 and *not* do all of these things was patently absurd.

We may assess the new academic bourgeoisie that began to dominate academic departments and institutes after the war by a perspective borrowed from Thorstein Veblen. Instead of "conspicuous consumption" as the hallmark of affluence, we may refer to *conspicuous research*. Ordinary research was not enough. It must be made conspicuous not merely through sheer bulk of project, but through one's conspicuous exemption from all ordinary academic activities. One must first be exempted from teaching, or from a significant share of teaching. Those who only taught were anything but members of the new bourgeoisie on the campus. One must also obtain, if possible, a title—whether Director or Research Professor—that made plain beyond all possible doubt that one's teaching was as minimal as one's research was maximal.

It is no wonder that there was a very noticeable blurring of the outlines of the academic image of the historic professor-exemplar to youth. For the member of the new bourgeoisie, in whatever sector of the university, engaged more and more typically in activities that took him frequently not only from classroom but from campus, was increasingly visible, proudly visible, as *professional* psychologist or mathematician or physicist rather than as professor in an academic institution. He was more and more commonly resident in some institute or center office than in an academic department office. Indeed, his prestige came in substantial degree from this very fact. He was equipped with a staff of technicians and clerks of a size sufficient to frighten away all but foundation executives, and seemed to be always just leaving or just returning to the campus, rather than being on it. It was more and more difficult for such individuals not to look like civil servants or businessmen rather than the professor-scholars that students had left home to study under.

It was once said that there was more difference between two professors, one of whom was an administrator, than between two administrators, one of whom was a professor. No doubt there are places in the academic world today where that is still true. But the Last Reformation has made it a great deal less true than it once was. The new bourgeoisie on the American campus saw to that.

Marx and Engels wrote: "The bourgeoisie has stripped of its halo every occupation hitherto honored and looked up to with reverent awe. It has converted the physician, the lawyer, the priest, the poet, the man of science, into its paid wage-laborers. The bourgeoisie has torn away from the family its sentimental veil, and has reduced the family relation to a mere money relation."

Thus the famous Marxian description of the transition of European society from status to contract, from patriarchalism to economism, from aristocracy to bourgeois democracy, from *Gemeinschaft* to *Gesellschaft*—or, as noted in title of this chapter, the rise of the new bourgeoisie. One need but change a very few of the words in the passage by Marx and Engels to make it remarkably appropriate to the American university in the quarter-century following World War II.

A great deal of the weakness of academic structure that the student revolts of the 1960s highlighted for the first time came directly from the kinds of role conflicts, blurrings of identity, and psychological tensions directly caused by the eruption of the new bourgeoisie. Even leaving to one side the student revolutionists, whose real object was and is, not university so much as surrounding political and economic systems, a very large number of nonrevolutionary students could not avoid being seriously disillusioned by a scene that proved to be, not community but corporation, led not by aristocrats but businessmen of the mind.

THE CULT OF INDIVIDUALITY

FOURTH AMONG THE MAJOR influences that have led to the degradation of the academic dogma is the astonishing eruption of the cult of the individual within the American university during the last two or three decades. As with respect to the higher capitalism, the advent of the new men of power, and the profound shift within the university from *Gemeinschaft* to *Gesellschaft,* we are dealing here with something remarkably akin to the Reformation of the sixteenth and seventeenth centuries in Europe. Then, in church principally, there was to be seen a momentous shift of emphasis from the corporate and liturgical to the individual; from the authority of the ecclesiastical community to the self-resident, self-generated authority of individual conscience, of, above all, individual faith. It is faith, not works, not memberships, not learning, not rules followed for their own sake, but faith alone that will win salvation for man. So thundered Luther and a host of other Protestant revolutionaries.

And so, in effect, thunder the apostles of the New Education, of academic Protestantism, today on the American cam-

pus. We have grown accustomed in recent years to the
demands of students for a "relevant" and "meaningful" education in the university; for liberation from intellectual requirements—including examinations, book lists, grades, and assignments; and for what is widely termed a new dedication to
the student, his needs, his identity, his ego, his peace of mind.
In certain ways it is all very much like the demands of a
rising number of persons in the whole sphere of religion, after
Luther and Calvin, for a faith that was relevant, meaningful,
intellectually undemanding, as free from sacrament and works
as possible, and committed, not so much to God, much less
Church, but to the imagined needs of the individual human
soul.

Just as there were rather weird cults in Protestant Christianity, and have been down to the present moment—some
of them reaching the rank of churches, self-styled anyhow,
with individual serenity of soul their highest objective, higher
even than dedication to God—so are there some rather weird
cults—call them schools, colleges, and programs—on the
American campus at the present time. They range from silent
communion in the forms of sensitivity, encounter, and "feel"
courses run by students all the way to entire new colleges
within universities, even whole campuses, dedicated to helping
the student solve what is fashionably known as "identity
crises."

Curriculum is regarded in such places in much the same
way sacraments and liturgy were regarded by early, zealous
Protestants: unnecessary to those with grace and unavailing
to those without it. Today use *identity* in place of grace. Just
as the more ethereal, self-obsessed, serenity-seeking forms of
Protestant Christianity have tended always to appeal most to

the moderately affluent, the heart of the modern middle class, so do the kinds of education I speak of here have greatest appeal to the children of the white middle class. I shall come back to this point a little later in the chapter. For now it is enough to stress the fact that what I here call the cult of individuality, in its rather bizarre forms, ranging from so-called liberal arts courses and colloquia to the more extreme variants of sensitivity, soul-discovering, and encounter classes, is overwhelmingly a movement addressed to the problem of relieving middle-class white children in the universities from the boredom, loneliness, and guilt their American upbringing has so often instilled in them.

"This place is so good to us," one student is quoted on a magnificent campus of one of the world's great universities, "there are times we suspect it's a subtly disguised insane asylum for freaks. Nobody hassles you—everybody listens. Man, that's therapy, not education." So it may be. But the line between therapy and education is becoming a much harder one to draw these days in the American university and college. And it is astonishing how quickly faculty fall into line with this whole view. Here is the faculty head of the educational policy committee on the same campus: "Perhaps we shouldn't have to baby-sit the identity crisis of our students, but they come to us scarred by education, in a state of suppressed rage, so crammed with facts and pushed to compete for grades that they've no idea who they are or why they should think." [1]

---

[1] The quotations are from the newsmagazine *Life,* May 8, 1970, in an article on the Santa Cruz campus of the University of California. The reporter declares that this campus was founded for the purpose of dealing with young people "who simultaneously demand total freedom and a recognition that they deserve a place in society." The

We are dealing here with a movement that began in the late 1940s with the Harvard Report on General Education in the vanguard. True, there was nothing in this report or in any of the other reports, manifestoes, and declarations on the needs of the student—always the student considered, one would believe from reading them, for the first time in history, as the *whole student,* the *personality*—about sensitivity, encounter, or identity crisis. But it is impossible to miss, in a whole variety of ways in the late 1940s and the 1950s, the national sweep of the cult of individuality and of the liberal arts crusade and, also, the sheer intensity of the efforts that could be seen everywhere being made.

I think it is important to emphasize this aspect of the academic scene in the decade of the 1950s. One of the repeated charges by students and faculty members alike during the student revolts of the following decade was that the universities and colleges had for a great many years persisted in a single mold, insensitive alike to the needs of students and to radical developments in the social order. But the fact is, no decade in the history of American higher education—with the possible exception of the first decade in the century, when so many colleges became universities in the German manner— was so rich in curricular change as the decade of the 1950s. Overnight, faculty members, usually, to be sure, under the leadership of administrators, were concerning themselves with revamping curriculum, seeking proper substitute for the old classical pattern and, at one and the same time, refuge for students from the winds of professionalism and research

characterization may or may not be true of Santa Cruz, but it is true of a great many programs currently burgeoning in the American academic scene. "Back to kindergarten today; tommorrow to the womb!" So might students in such programs chorus.

capitalism in the university. Everywhere the purpose of the liberal arts-based reforms was declared to be the individual.

It may be asked: has not the purpose of education always been the individual and his needs? Has it not been said, from the beginning of the history of the university, that from the proper study of the disciplines individuals acquire strengths not previously possessed? Did not the British government, through all the greatness of the Empire, go to Oxford and Cambridge for the men of leadership, moral stamina, and imagination it wanted? The answers to all of these questions are, of course, in the affirmative. But affirmative only in a distinctive and special sense. And this sense is best expressed by use again of the word "indirect." In the same way that the university's traditional service to society was indirect—expressed, as we have seen, through its teaching of individuals and prosecution of scholarship adapted to this teaching—so was the university's commitment to the individual student indirect.

We can state the matter this way: under the academic dogma, the knowledge that was accumulated and transmitted in the university was, in a real sense, its own reason for being. No other reason had to be manufactured. But at one and the same time there was widespread belief that students, in their assiduous and disciplined pursuit of this knowledge, would inevitably sharpen intellectual powers and discover mental energies not previously known. And, along with this belief or realization, went another almost equally important: that students, by rubbing shoulders with one another especially, but also with faculty at least to some extent, would similarly sharpen moral and social aptitudes. Both the intellectual and the moral development of the individual student were, in other words, aspects of the traditional academic community, stated nowhere more eloquently than by Newman in his *Idea of the University* and by the great Jowett at Balliol in countless utterances. This conception of the function of learning is to be found in the whole Western tradition, from Plato to Whitehead and Dewey. Mind, character, and individuality, all of these are clearly beneficiaries of the pursuit of knowledge, no matter how abstruse or remote from present-day concerns this knowledge may be.

But in the same way that the character and mission of the university are decisively changed when the university's service to the social order is declared to be direct instead, so is the character of the curriculum decisively changed when the purpose becomes the direct, instead of indirect, cultivation of individuality or personality. To believe that the individual's moral as well as mental being is enriched by the assiduous study of Chaucer or Ralph Ellison, of Aristotle or Sartre, of Marx or Dewey—or, for that matter by patient work in the scientific laboratory—is one thing. It is something decidedly different when cultivation of individuality is made the direct function of the university or of the liberal arts. Different, certainly, so far as the nature of the curriculum and also the nature of the academic dogma are concerned.

For now a different set of criteria can be, and generally have to be, employed for the worthiness of subject matter in curriculum, for the relevance of what is being taught. If the direct function of the college is to develop individuality, a great deal that has traditionally gone into curriculum can be regarded as irrelevant and expendable. Reformers cannot help but think that there are far more effective ways of getting to the heart of the objective than by courses in the humanities, social sciences, and natural sciences, all of which are chosen, organized, and taught in terms of criteria arising ultimately from the disciplines themselves.

So was it thought in the Reformation when Protestant reformers went to work on the whole intermediate structure of liturgy, sacrament, and sacred learning in the Church. If the objective of religion is purification of man's soul and if this is best achieved by direct encounter of God and man, then the intervening structures of corporate authority and cumulative, corporate wisdom can be and should be abolished. So thought many a Protestant in the sixteenth and seventeenth centuries. Everyman his own priest was a widely cherished doctrine. Purity of faith was the touchstone of the new religion, and in the light of this revolutionary doctrine, mere learning, mere erudition or mastery of a sacred discipline came to seem not merely irrelevant but an actual hindrance to the pursuit of grace.

In the seventeenth century Bacon and Descartes extended the implications of Protestant stress upon Everyman to all knowledge. No present-day protagonist of the New Left in the universities or advocate of encounter and sensitivity classes could be more withering in contempt for the traditional curriculum, for the amassed learning of the several academic disciplines, than Bacon and Descartes were toward the traditional learning of schoolmen and philosophers. Bacon's emphasis on method—in his case experimental method —was expressly for the purpose of bringing true knowledge within the immediate reach of Everyman, of removing it from the privileged sphere of scholars and priests. So too was Descartes' emphasis on method, which in his *Discourse* turned out to be the method of, first, skepticism toward all that is known and, second, the direct employment of common sense. All men are equal, thought Descartes, in common sense, and this alone, by working rigorously in accord with the simple rules of logic, suffices to bring knowledge, that is, true knowledge, relevant knowledge, within the direct reach of Everyman. As Luther and Calvin by their emphasis upon pristine faith made the hierarchy of sacred learning irrelevant, so Bacon and Decartes by their emphasis upon pristine reason, upon the sense and sensibility common to all men, made the hierarchy of sacred and secular learning alike irrelevant. All men are equal.

In the century following Descartes and Bacon, their method, and particularly that aspect of the method that Descartes had stressed, passed into the general currency of philosophical and political thought. What, after all, do we find in Rosseau's works but extension of Lutheranism and Cartesianism to each and every sector of society. Whether in the first *Discourse,* in *Emile,* in *La nouvelle Heloise,* or in the momentous *Social Contract,* what we find, diversely employed, is the dogma of Everyman: Everyman his own moralist, his own teacher, his own sage, and, above all, his own ruler. Just as had Luther and Calvin, and then Bacon and Descartes, Rousseau subjected the traditional learning of Western Europe to the acids of his individualism and his equalitarianism. Beneath the homespun of the peasant and laborer lies a truer morality, he argued, than beneath the raiment of either courtier or academician. And also, as Rousseau pounded home on many an occasion, a truer intellect and knowledge.

What I have called the cult of individuality in the contemporary university is, then, no newer in Western history than the capitalism and the uprooting of traditional authority we have already examined. In the same way that academic capitalism and its allied patterns of new power have had a fragmenting effect on the traditional academic structure of authority, so has the revived emphasis upon individual grace, individual faith, and individual development had a profoundly atomizing effect upon the traditional academic community. The cry for relevance by the student left in the 1960s is scarcely more, it would seem, than the cry of Protestants, of Cartesians, and of Rousseauians for relevance and for a dismantling of traditional, corporate learning in the earlier Reformation.

Within the contemporary university, the cult of individuality seems to have had its first manifestation in the tidal wave of adulation for the liberal arts that rolled over academia at about the same time that the new capitalism was threatening the structure of the university. It was almost as though in the worship of the liberal arts many a project titan or entrepreneur was salving his soul. Rarely, during this period, was the referent of "liberal arts" the medieval trivium or quadrivium, or any of the learned disciplines within the humanities such as philosophy, history, literature, or language. By an act of legerdemain this term came to apply to a kind of mishmash of snippets from the traditional disciplines. An earlier emphasis at Columbia College on Great Books became in time an emphasis on what many called Great Snippets.

Giving grace and meaning to the new enterprise was the emphasis on the individual student and his asserted "needs." A host of faculty committees from Harvard, under Conant, all the way across the country, in large universities and in small undergraduate colleges, began the awesome task of

passing upon these "needs." The word "experimental" became talismanic, and woe to any academic institution during
this period that could not point to this or that "experimental"
course within its walls. The terms "liberal arts," "experimental," "survey," and, eventually, "integrated" all became
approximately interchangeable in the early 1950s. The re-
making of curricula, the redesigning of graduation requirements, the reinterpretation of the mission of the college, such
endeavors were rife during the 1950s in the United States.
The air was filled with newly discovered excellences in tiny
colleges—no matter how primitive in resources and mediocre
in faculty and student minds—throughout the country. First-
rate colleges such as that at Chicago, along with the Swarth-
mores, Reeds, and Antiochs, were found to have quite extraordinary records in the number of their graduates who went
on to graduate school, to eminence in the sciences, and by
some kind of nonsequitur, this extraordinary record was
deemed the result of integrated courses in the humanities and
social sciences rather than of the family background and high
intelligence of the students themselves—or of some highly
specialized learning experience that each of the students was
bound to have had somewhere in his undergraduate career.
No one, however, during these years was likely to look with
favor on any kind of specialization. "General" was, along
with the terms noted above, a word of high prestige.
Specialists in generalism were all over the scene, and in many
institutions so-called general colleges were to be seen: successors to the hoary colleges of letters, arts, and sciences.

But however "general," however committed to Great Books
or Great Snippets, however broad the range of knowledge
crammed into one or other of the multitude of survey or in-

tegrated courses that could be seen mushrooming in academic United States in the period 1945–1960, the raison d'être was invariably and dedicatedly the individual. The individual student, it was said, nay, trumpeted everywhere, has certain clearly identifiable needs. Only by meeting these needs directly could the student be prepared adequately for his role as citizen, as provider or homemaker, as proper member of the social order. There was the need for breadth of knowledge, for rigor of thinking, for moral and social tolerance, for ability to adapt to a changing world; these were some of the needs in the individual student that faculty committees on reform of curriculum perennially discovered and rediscovered.

Let us not doubt the reality of the needs. Either today or yesterday or tomorrow. Stated abstractly, they can scarcely be repudiated. How to meet these abstractly, committee-formulated, definable needs was, however, another matter. The late Reformation in Europe could have been no more profuse in religious cults than the American academic scene was in what can only be called liberal arts cults in the 1950s. From Harvard to Berkeley, from Amherst to Reed, curricular reform was in the air, and the talismanic word everywhere was the "student." In the student's interest, his *direct* interest, a new curricular community would be designed to take the place of the old classical education.

Many of these liberal arts constructions were ingenious in their design. And if they were as likely as not to be forgotten a very few years after their inception in any given college, the fault lay not so much in the often admirable design as it did in the immense difficulty of persuading first-rate minds to engage in the teaching that these reformed curricula called for and, for those who managed to be persuaded, to give their energies and time as the ideals of the reformed curricula demanded. Over and over during the last couple of decades faculty members have produced revolutionary plans for curricula and experimental colleges. But over and over the same faculty members have manifested little interest in participating in what they have created. The best, all too often, flee, their curricular passion spent in the design; the worst stay on to engage in endless curriculum-tinkering or rearrangement of liberal arts icons. This is not the complete picture of the academic scene, but no one who has lived on an American campus, especially a university campus, during the past quarter century will doubt the considerable truth in what I have just written.

The principal fault of the new curricula and programs, from the point of view of the typical faculty member, is the vast amount of time they require in teaching and in perpetual shoring-up of faith. The traditional academic department, with all its faults, was at least a practical answer to the problem of reconciling the ordinary faculty member's desire for teaching with his desire for resarch. Housekeeping responsibilities require a certain amount of committee work, but this tends to be rather small in amount compared with what is typically demanded by one of the reformed curricula, a model program, or college. The late Heywood Broun, himself a Socialist, once said that the greatest single weakness of socialism was the number of meetings it required. Something of this colors the average faculty member's attitude toward curricular experimentation and reform. He tends to be for it in principle but to shrink from the number of meetings—and classes and small seminars and hours of special studies— which have ever been the price of the cult of individuality, whether in its Protestant or its academic form.

From the liberal arts cults of the 1950s it was really but a short step to the kinds of encounter, sensitivity, and individuality courses that exist today, one of the products of the 1960s. Their number is still small relatively, but it is growing, and there can be little doubt of their appeal to the kind of student who predominates on the American campus.

He is overwhelmingly middle class. And one of the consequences of being middle class in origin today is having become used to a vast amount of attention and a vast amount of love—instant love—in one's home. The parent-child tie is clearly the most intense tie in the contemporary family structure of the American middle class. The child is accustomed to being loved and, above all, *he is accustomed to being listened to:* at the dinner table, in the automobile when being driven to one or other of the multitude of dens, packs, and clubs middle-class American children belong to. So great is the average middle-class child's dependence upon both love and being listened to that going off to college can sometimes be a traumatic experience for him—and also her, for I see no significant difference here between the sexes.

I do not say that this is a fixed and permanent characteristic of the middle class. I think it is a rather stronger trait in America than in Europe, and considerably stronger today, of course, than it was in earlier generations in this country. But of its present and likely-to-continue importance, there can be no real question.

Middle-class children do not like the experience of being ignored by their elders, and they do not like the experience of being left alone either. Being alone is a nearly frightening experience for the middle-class child of even college age; and being bored, or easily becoming bored, is a very common experience. One may say that the middle-class child is always on the brink of boredom, saved only by the incessant attentions which have been his lot at home. Hence the ever rising demand on college campuses today for classes of a type that permit not only the strong sense of "togetherness," of youthful community, but also the constant opportunity to be heard, to participate in the planning and the implementation of courses. The middle-class student at college today is affluent generally, but he is *psychologically needy*. The vast burgeoning during the 1950s of psychological welfare agencies on the campus, operating out of the offices—empires, one might say —of deans of students, is testimony to the increased demand for, downright need for, attention of the sort he was accustomed to getting at home.

But welfare agencies are never adequate. What we are witnessing today is the transfer of psychological functions from the dean of students' office to the classroom and undergraduate seminar. There is every reason to suppose that students getting their due share of attention in an encounter or sensitivity class will be less prone than other students to go to the dean for psychological aid.

It is easy to see mere banality, mere escape from loneliness, mere assertion of some herd instinct, in these encounter types of course, program, and—at one university—entire college. But the relation of these types to the liberal arts curricula of the 1950s should not be missed. As I have emphasized, they were primarily concerned, though usually with considerable tincture of a genuine great-books interest, with student needs, with the asserted needs of the individual student. Then, these needs were commonly set forth in terms of the responsibilities of citizenship, of leadership, of moral distinctiveness. But the crucial referent was nonetheless the individual.

The present phase of what I have called the cult of individuality is plainly much more radical. Like secondary and more intense phases of certain Reformation religious cults, this one carries with it almost total abnegation of traditional text or academic liturgy. The equal blessedness of all souls in the cult is assumed and, where necessary, preached with zeal. Equality of student and teacher is as much a matter of dogma as equality of communicant and preacher was (and is) in radical Protestant sects. Whereas the first phase of the cult of individuality, the liberal arts phase, declared *disciplinary* knowledge expendable, even injurious, the present and more radical phase declares *all knowledge*—knowledge, that is, in the traditional university sense—expendable, injurious, and, in the word of the hour, irrelevant.

🌿 9 🌿

THE DELUGE OF
HUMANITARIANISM

THE UNIVERSITY IS properly concerned with service to society. At its best it has always been in the thick of things. No mistake could be greater than confusing the purpose of the university with that of the monastery. Both the university and the monastery are products of the Middle Ages, and not infrequently they have resembled one another in actual practice. Certainly, a good deal of the scholarship of the Middle Ages, especially in the early period, was connected with the monastery. Scholarship remains a function of many monastic orders. And there have been times when the university, by taking refuge in a more or less ritually protected curriculum, has been more like a retreat from society than an institution that has service to society as its fundamental function. Nevertheless, from the time the university began as an institution in Bologna and Paris its mission has been that of service, not retreat or pure contemplation.

But this service has been, until very recently, overwhelmingly indirect service. By this I mean only that the university has been, ever since its founding, a means of preparing individuals—that is, students—for the places in the social order where unusual skill or learning is required. We call these the professions, and as I have repeatedly noted in this book the relation between the university and the professions has always been a close one. No greater fallacy concerning the university is imaginable than that of supposing it to be, historically, a mere haven for the liberal arts and for individuals of contemplative mind or of monastic inclination alone. From the founding of the university in Bologna and Paris around the professional areas of theology, law, and medicine down to the American university that is today so rich in professional schools, covering a large number of social needs, there is a straight line. Even in the historic English universities, Oxford and Cambridge, where by virtue of their residential colleges professional schools did not have the existence and luster that these had on the Continent, the relation between the university and society—the British civil service, clergy, and other spheres—was a close one.

But I repeat: the university's service to society has always tended to be indirect; to be seen in terms of the university's preparation of individuals, that is, the students, to go forth and directly serve the more important, the widely recognized, needs of the social order. Only rarely prior to the present age did the university engage forthrightly and directly in the meeting of the technical and professional needs of the economic, political, and social order. And because of this, because of the indirectness of service, because such service was defined in the terms of the university's residual functions, teaching and scholarship, no significant conflict existed between these functions and the university's service to the social order. I say "no significant conflict." The history of the university is, of course, filled with controversies and conflicts at any given time as to whether a given skill in society was suitable for incorporation in the university curriculum. The controversy attending curricula and schools in fields such as social work and librarianship within memory of many of us has abundant precedent in the eight centuries of the university's history. The two great English universities never saw fit to accept even law and medicine. This is all true enough. My point, however, is that once a professional skill was accepted, for good or bad, in the university, it was accepted in terms of its conversion into a body of teaching, represented by curriculum, and into the beginnings of a body of scholarship. Service to society remained indirect.

Few things, however, are more spectacular about the contemporary American university than its plunge into direct service to society: to agriculture, business, government—local, state, and federal—social welfare, environmental control, middle-class leisure needs, and most recently, the whole, infinitely delicate and mine-strewn field of ethnic uplift—from Harlem across the country to Watts.

I am well aware that such words as those I have written will seem to many the pitiful laments of one losing his cushioned ivory tower. *What,* deny the limitless resources of our great universities to those in society who plainly need them? Are not the people of Watts, of Harlem, of other ethnic enclaves as entitled to the succor of the university as are middle-class white farmers, middle-class white labor union members, the lords of Pentagon, of HEW, and of all the other principalities of government, not to mention the vast numbers of middle-class whites who send their children at low cost to such a university as the University of California? No doubt other, even more outraged questions are possible here.

To them all I can only offer sympathy. I honor the ethical motivations of the university in its humanitarian labors. And I particularly honor the motivations of those most recent of the university's labors directed toward the disadvantaged in our society.

But my aim in this volume is solely to try to account for the degradation of the academic dogma and for the fragmentation of the academic community. I would be happy if it were possible to single out only the manifestly evil as the cause of this degradation and fragmentation.

That, however, is not possible. For any clear view of the academic crisis at the present time is obliged to include *all* impacts upon the academic community, upon the academic dogma: those as appealing in their aim as the university's organized efforts to help the poverty-stricken and ethnically disadvantaged as well as those unprepossessing efforts to help Pentagon, CIA, wealthy businessmen and farmers, and all-white, middle-class labor unions. There is no end to the number of the miserable, the downtrodden, the alienated, the precariously situated, and the otherwise needy members of American society. The middle-class housewife is lonely: she must be helped by university-sponsored courses designed to relieve her loneliness through perhaps the reading of Great Books, or if not the reading, the hearing about them. The businessman is in incessant need of counsel or insight that will help him surmount the obstacle of competition. The farmer is in constant need of better fertilizers, insecticides, and harvesters to help him in his praiseworthy endeavor to make life more secure. Labor union leaders can use all the advice they can get in the monumental task of keeping their rank and file happy and, at the same time, remaining in communication with employers. Our cities, we are told, have become jungles. Our air, water, and land have become polluted. Our transportation system on the ground is clearly in a condition approximating rigor mortis. Automobiles need to be made safer, beauty parlors more efficiently operated, banks and real estate firms more profitable.

So it goes. Society is a huge complex of problems, discontents, and needs ranging all the way from the merely critical to the desperate. Hardly an issue of the newspaper or of one's favorite magazine does not illuminate the plight of some needy group, be it real estate brokers at bay or mine workers faced with technological displacement. Nor, seemingly, do the problems and needs diminish with time among the groups that have longest had the university's assistance.

Agriculture was the first major group in American society to receive the university's humanitarian assistance. It is both interesting and important to my argument here to observe, however, that the university's approach to the problem of agricultural assistance was indirect, not direct. A whole new system (I am referring here, of course, only to the great state universities and colleges that participated at all in rendering service to agriculture) was devised: the Agricultural Extension. Related to, it was yet sharply distinct from, the departments of agricultural science on the campus. There was genius in this from the point of view of the farmers themselves. The counsel that came to them from the scientific departments was mediated, as it were, by an organization staffed with people capable of absorbing directly the scientific knowledge and then of communicating it effectively to the farmers themselves.

But there was also genius in the system from the point of view of the university. No set of activities, however worthy, however vital to the nation, could, under this system, compete with or distract from the primacy of teaching and research or scholarship on the campus. There was recognition of the needs of agriculture, yes, but there was also recognition of the needs of the university itself—of students and of faculty members on the campus—and of the fragility that has ever lain in the academic dogma.

The principle of intermediation continued for a long time in the university in America with respect to these humanitarian services. What was first done for agriculture became, in time, a reality for a slowly rising number of other groups in society. What is called University Extension is also a means of extending benefits of the university to nonuniversity elements of the public. University faculty members may, and often do, participate in it. At the start, few taught in University Extension systems who were not bona fide members of the university involved. But their identities in the Extension were meticulously distinct from their identities in the university proper. And for excellent reason. Standards, content, objectives, ages and types of student, all of these differed substantially from one system to the other. Again, we are obliged to honor the motives of those who, wishing to respond to clamant public needs, yet maintained the academic community and its needs on the campus. Whether it was the agricultural experiment station many miles out from the campus in the country or the extension center in the downtown areas, the sanctity of the campus was maintained.

But within the past quarter of a century the structure of the university's humanitarian functions in society has changed decisively. Less and less, now, is the principle of intermediation employed. Even in the instances I have just described, it is possible to observe, I think, a weakening of the principle, a blurring of the distinction that once seemed vital in the university. But such weakening is nothing as compared with the frank abandonment of the principle in the large number of humanitarian functions today performed by the university. Increasingly, one finds the academic department itself made the vehicle of direct humanitarian service. Along with its prime teaching and other academic functions are to be found those pertaining to some sector of society in need.

It is not only the weakening or disappearance of the principle of intermediation. It is the constantly rising volume of requests made by groups outside. First agriculture, then the middle class, interested in leisure-time study, then business, then labor. Then others and others. And finally came, as we know, the sufficient strength of the poor and the black and the brown, who have managed to win recognition of their problems by the university. Aid stations for the needy ethnic began to sit at respectful distance from aid stations for the needy farmer, the businessman, the government chief, and the labor executive. And why not?

The president of a great state university has declared the prime mission of his university to be that of solving the urban problem. All resources of the university, he announces, will be made available in the onslaught against urban blight, urban violence, urban ethnic discrimination, urban illiteracy, and so on. Why not? Why not also against urban boredom, urban alienation, urban use of narcotics, urban traffic jams, urban malaise of spirit? These are problems too. And, beyond doubt, there are professors at all levels in the university, in all departments and schools and colleges, who can render some kind of assistance to the economically, politically, morally, and psychologically needy. Even the Chaucerian scholar can do something: child sit, perhaps, for working mothers.

I don't want to lapse into the cynical or disparaging. All of these, and many other, problems do indeed exist: in city, in town, in hamlet, in factory, in brokerage house, and on farm, in mental institution, in primary school, and on playground. There are problems everywhere. And there is no question that on the faculties of our universities are men and women who know a great deal about the causes of these problems and their solution. They can help valiantly.

But they cannot help valiantly and at the same time do effectively that for which they were brought to the university in the first place. That is, teach and engage in scholarship, in the preparation of students whose mission will be, assuming personal inclination and will, the direct meeting of one or other of the nearly limitless range of social problems in our society. May I again stress what I said at the beginning of this chapter: I do not see the university as some kind of monastic retreat, least of all as an aristocratic enclave built upon indifference to the needs of the social order. I am willing to declare indeed: if there is no possible way by which the university can help our society meet its problems, then by all means abandon it. The university is far too expensive an operation for support, by taxpayer or donor, of mere adolescent socialization, of glorified sitting.

But is there no merit in the kind of service that is, and meticulously remains, indirect? That is, the service involved in the educating of engineers, businessmen, librarians, social workers, physicians, and others; rather than the kind of service that involves the university's mobilizing itself into a direct assault on the problems of urban blight, smog, and boredom? I shall indicate in a later chapter some of the reasons why the university, by reason of structure and character, is peculiarly unfitted for very many of these assaults upon evironmental social problems. Now, all I want to do is stress what seems to me the obvious fact that if the university rides off in all directions at once it will hardly go anywhere. How could it?

More concretely, how, as a simple problem in logistics, is it possible for the university to deal with all or even most of the social and political problems that cry out for attention today and, at the same time, deal with those vital functions of teaching and research, at levels appropriate to the university, which, if they are to get discharged at all in our society today, will have to be discharged in the university?

I do not see any alternative to the view that among the influences of the past quarter-century that have led to the degradation of the academic dogma and the fragmentation of the academic community, the deluge of humanitarianism is among the greatest. There is simply no way by which a community can be built around the vital functions of teaching, learning, and scholarship—in all those areas and fields that our society properly regards as important—and, at the same time, make its members available, through department, school, institute, and project, for any and all the needs of the social order that at any given moment are likely today to be thrust upon the university.

There is one final aspect of all this that is worthy of emphasis. I am concerned in this book with the forces and influences which have led to the degradation of the academic dogma in contemporary America, to the diminution of the status of the university and what it stands for. Nothing so diminishes the regard in which either a person or an institution is held by others as that person's or institution's all too eager willingness to assume responsibilities to which insufficient or inept resources are brought. In part it has been the university's earned prestige in the scholarly and scientific disciplines that has brought a long line of governmental, political, economic, and social supplicants to its doors, begging for solution to their problems. In part, alas, this long line today is, however, the result of the university's false representation of its abilities and resources. To take on, voluntarily or involuntarily, a social problem for direct action—such as environmental purification or ethnic uplift—where the difficulties are monumental and where failure of objective is almost predictable can hardly fail to lead to disillusionment on the part of the public and, then, to unwillingness to regard the university highly for the things it *can* do well.

❦ 10 ❧

THE POLITICIZATION
OF THE UNIVERSITY

THE FINAL, and in many ways the crucial, manifestation
of the university's Reformation during the past quarter-century is its extreme politicization. There are many ways of
showing this: the ever closer relation of the university to the
federal government through the multitudinous contracts and
projects that the universities took on; the dislodgment or
erosion of many of the time-created immunities and auton-
omies of the university within the larger political order; the
rising intensity of national political issues assimilated into the
halls of the university and made into divisive *university*
political issues; the slowly rising belief on the part of many
faculty members that the university must take, *as the university,* an active role in politics; and, along with these more
obvious examples of politicization, the steady increase through
the 1950s and 1960s of that adversary type of relationship,
one founded on the utilization of litigation, which one en-
counters wherever traditional, consensual relationships are

137

undergoing severe change. This last point is an important one.

Politicization is one of the clearest indicators of change. Studies by anthropologists and sociologists, as well as historians, attest to this. Whether we are dealing with a primitive culture undergoing what we call modernization, a period such as the sixteenth and seventeenth centuries in Western Europe, or the contemporary university, we invariably find an upthrust of political behavior, of litigation, of adversary relationships to be a highly visible accompaniment of social, economic, and intellectual change. Traditional roles and statuses either become weakened in their effect or else they begin to take on more and more of the hue of politics. More and more issues arise that, it is widely believed, are either themselves basically political issues or subject only to political ajudication in the long run. Adversary groups resembling political followings or even parties begin to appear. A more or less permanent structuring into a political left, a right, and a center comes into being. Each of these serves as a kind of filter through which all issues pass before they are assimilated by their individual members in attitudes, beliefs and ideologies.

It was this way in the Western Europe that began to form when the traditional authority of the Roman Catholic Church had been broken. Then too a class of *politiques* arose—the most profound of which were, of course, Bodin, Hobbes, Locke, and Rousseau—who gave to politics all the dedication and intensity that earlier philosophers and intellectuals had given to the Church. It is this way in many parts of Asia and Africa today where, with colonial rule withdrawn or destroyed and with ancient structures of clan, tribe, and village manifestly inadequate, as the consequence of dislocation of function and crumbling of belief, a new class of politicians and political administrators is rapidly emerging.

Much the same kind of politicization can be seen occurring in the American university in the period immediately following World War II. The causes are varied. Many of them are embedded in the kinds of change we have already considered, for, is I have just noted, convulsive social and economic change always leads to a marked increase in politics. But some of the causes are to be found not in the university as such but rather in the character of American politics during the period and in the university's necessarily close relation to national politics.

I am certainly not suggesting that political behavior on the part of academics was utterly new to the university in this period. Far from it. Those of us who were on the American campus in the 1930s are not likely to have forgotten the high intensity of political support of causes then. The issues of Depression, capitalism, fascism, socialism, and communism were all burning issues. Anyone who thinks that either students or faculty members eschewed politics in that earlier decade is utterly uninformed. I have no reliable figures at hand, but I would confidently venture the guess that proportionately far more students were then declared members of radical political organizations than was the case in the 1960s. One could say the same, I think, about faculty members. If there were known Maoists, in any serious sense, at all among faculty members in the 1960s, their number must have been infinitesimal. But more than a mere handful of faculty members in the 1930s were Communists, or moved very closely with the Communist party.

Even apart from the extreme left literally hundreds, perhaps thousands of faculty and students in the 1930s, became, possibly for the first time in their lives, ardent New Dealers or Progressives. Rare, as I well recall, was the faculty club lunch table not seized by discussion of domestic political issues and, then, of international issues. Politics was indeed a strong current on the American campus in the 1930s, and it is fair to say that a certain *radicalization* of the faculty took place. That is, the number of those who identified with the left, with the cause of humanitarian liberalism in however tepid intensity, grew constantly. The Depression saw to that.

None of this is to be doubted. And yet I do not think that the university as such became politicized during this earlier period. My aim here is not to praise the old radical anymore than it is to criticize the new radical—the new faculty radical of the 1950s or the new student radical of the 1960s. I am interested only in the comparative impact of each thrust of radicalism on the university and the academic community. For argument's sake, I am willing to stipulate that the old radical was as destructive in intent as the new: as sworn an enemy of all civilized values, all freedoms, all authorities. And there is certainly no question that the radicalism of the 1930s had a far more decisive impact upon government than anything we can find in the 1950s or 1960s. I mean *positive* impact, guiding impact in many forms, including even those clandestine forms that were to be the subjects of trials and hearings in the late 1940s.

Still, the university was not notably politicized in the 1930s. This is the important point for present purposes. The national issues, the national lines of ideology, the national cleavages may have been, as indeed they were, reflected on the campus. They did not, however, often become translated into curricular issues, academic ideologies, and faculty, *qua* faculty, cleavages. Perhaps some of this occurred here and there. Perhaps decisions on strictly curricular or other academic matters were now and then reached through struggle by forces whose real and substantial nature came from views regarding Soviet communism. There must have been some of this, especially in New York, Chicago, and the San Francisco Bay area—all of them historic centers of political radicalism. By comparison, however, with what was to exist in the 1950s and 1960s, it was small in scope and mild in intensity. It is with no intent of lauding the Old Left that I can report from considerable personal experience with it that it did not seek to remake, much less destroy, the university: only capitalism and bourgeois culture! [1]

Very different was the faculty radicalism of the 1950s. And, it goes without emphasis, the faculty and student radicalism of the 1960s. What we find in this period, beginning markedly in the late 1940s among faculty members in universities across the country, was a steadily growing politicization of *academic* issues. Since the period 1945–1960 is so commonly treated today by historians as an essentially quiescent period, politically speaking, I think it is important to emphasize that among faculties at least in this country it was a period of constantly growing political commitment, political zeal, and political ideology.

---

[1] Sidney Hook has made the correct and illuminating point that the radicalism of the 1930s sought to *de*politicize the university: to remove teaching and scholarship as far as possible from sectarian demands of the political order. It was autonomy from politics that radicals of the 1930s sought for curriculum and academic government.

Not only was the faculty of the 1950s much stronger in these qualities than had been the faculty of the 1930s, there was also—and this is the essential point of present discussion—far greater readiness to extend this commitment, zeal, and ideology, drawn from national and international politics, to the traditional academic matters that faculty members dealt with.

It is important to understand this aspect of the 1950s. There was a rising curve of both politicization and radicalization of university faculties in this country. Well before the student radicals of the 1960s went to work on the American campus, seeking to plunge the university into the mainstream of American politics, a good deal of their work had already been done by faculty members in the preceding decade.

This prior politicization was, of course, vital to the insurrections that took place on the university campus in the 1960s. Insurrections and revolutions in history are never the result solely of *negative* conditions: that is, poverty, oppression, differential wealth, and so forth. These provide soil, to be sure. But the fires of revolution have to be lighted by political torches; more specifically, by the ideas and techniques of those already political prepared. It is inconceivable to me that the Mario Savios and Tom Haydens and Mark Rudds could have ever been inspired to organize insurrections in the 1960s had not the way of insurrection—or at the very least the respectability of the insurrectionary way—been more or less established by faculty members earlier. Faculty members, let it be added quickly, who often proved to have little heart or stomach for events of the 1960s.

There are several pertinent reasons why the faculty in this

country should have become substantially radicalized, certainly politicized, during the late 1940s and the whole decade of the 1950s. There was the Hiss case, the spy trials generally, the establishment of the Independent Progressive party under Henry Wallace with its strong radical foundations drawn from the Soviet-oriented left, the occasional dismissals of Communists from schools and colleges, the long, strongly inflaming issue of loyalty oaths for teachers —with the fateful struggle over the oath at Berkeley a matter of obsessive concern to academics nationally—and the whole bitterly controverted issue of political tests of faculty qualification.

Above all, there was McCarthyism. No single figure, no single issue back in the 1930s had ever seized the minds of faculty members as did the person of Senator Joe McCarthy and the cause he represented in the 1950s. I would suppose that McCarthyism, above any other single force, had the effect of quickening the already proceeding radicalization of the American campus. For McCarthy's enemy, his declared enemy, was not labor, not labor unions, not the people—in the Populist sense—but almost strictly and exclusively the intellectuals in this country, academic intellectuals especially.

Given his assaults in so many intellectual areas, his challenging of the loyalty of intellectuals, his threats to "get" Harvard and other universities, it would be extraordinary if the mind of the American faculty had *not* become visibly radicalized in the 1950s: oriented generally toward civil rights matters and other issues within which the very survival of the university could be regarded as at stake. Nothing that came out of the fierce disputes of the 1930s, not even the almost religious hatred of fascism among liberals and radicals, ever transferred itself so completely to the halls of the university, ever attached itself, so to speak, to the very roles of academics, as did the threat of McCarthyism, as this threat was almost universally perceived by university faculty.

And, at opposite corner, stood the glowing presence of Adlai Stevenson. Not since Woodrow Wilson—if indeed he —had any political figure in American life so completely seized the faculty and intellectual mind in America. Himself something of a conservative in early views, the product of quasi-aristocratic lineage and breeding, Ivy League to the core, gifted in all the rhetorical and stylistic ways that are dear to intellectuals everywhere, Adlai Stevenson was the almost perfect polar opposite to Senator Joseph McCarthy. Each in a sense was the *indispensable* opposite of the other. Without both figures, it is unlikely, it seems to me, that that special and peculiarly intense seizure of the academic mind by politics, its zeal, dedication, and commitment, as well as its hatreds and animosities, could ever have taken place. From the academic scene McCarthy, representing the powers of Dark, and Stevenson, representing the powers of Light, were the nearly perfect incarnations of a kind of Zoroastrian political struggle, one that involved intimations of absolute good and of absolute evil.

In short, politicization and radicalization, as we see these in the 1950s in the parts of the campus where faculty members lived, had nearly impeccable roots. And that is precisely the point. Had the roots not been impeccable, had McCarthy not been the powerful and sinister figure he was, had Stevenson not been the gifted, almost beautiful mind that he was, it is hardly likely, I think, that the politicization

I write of here could have gotten much further than did the politicization of the 1930s. Not even toward fascism, it seems to me, did faculty members of the 1930s, even the most liberal of them, hold the kind of remorseless hate that faculty members came to feel almost universally toward McCarthyism. And, I should guess, with very good reason. Nor did President Roosevelt ever, at any point in his career, shine with the effulgence that Stevenson did for the academic intellectual.

The greatest difference, however, between the radicalism of the 1950s and that of the 1930s, so far as the faculty were involved, was simply that politics, in one form or other, entered into the very marrow of the university in America. Even if one had somehow managed to sleep through the Zoroastrian struggle between Stevenson and McCarthy, he could not have been oblivious to the fantastic increase in political behavior, in adversary relationships, and in academic litigation that took place during the decade.

The increase I speak of was far greater, as Seymour Lipset has notably emphasized, in the public than in the private universities. The Berkeley faculty, for example, was dominated by politics—internal and external—to a considerably greater degree than any of the Ivy League universities. The gulf between faculty and administration widened perceptibly in the public universities during the 1950s. If the gulf even existed at a Princeton or Harvard, it was not noticeable to the outsider. No one could miss it at a Berkeley, a Michigan, a Wisconsin, or a UCLA. Not until the mid-1960s would the Ivy League universities come to know this rift and, with it, the high degree of politicization, of radicalization, that the great public universities had known since at least 1950.

Politicization was also a product of the new capitalism on

the campus. So much of this economic affluence was governmental, notably federal, in source. The number and the complexity of university—including private university—relationships to political government could not help but increase under the weight of the innumerable contracts and projects that were funded by money over which, eventually, Congress had full control. Members of the student left in the 1960s spoke truly when they declared they were not the first to insinuate politics into the universities. That work, they properly argued, had already been done by agencies of government working directly with universities and with individual members of the faculty.

Still another manifestation of the higher degree of politicization found on the campus in the 1950s was the rise in what I can only call litigation. That is, formalized, more or less bureaucratized, ways of proceeding in curricular and other academic matters; ways that virtually demanded a kind of adversary relationship, however muted and civilized it might be. One found an ever increasing number of committees concerned with matters that a mere decade ago would have been dealt with, insofar as the matters themselves existed, through the highly informal modes of consensus that commonly existed in adcademic communities. The number of full-time administrators increased substantially in the universities, but so did the number of *faculty* preoccupations with academic-political issues. Indeed, in many places these became almost incessant. Again, it is useful to point out that what I am here writing about was far more noticeable in the public than in the private universities. The latter were, however, getting a preview of what would later befall them.

Interestingly, though not, I think, inexplicably, a considerable amount of faculty radicalism in the 1950s was to be found precisely within the new enclaves of wealth and power that were the substance of what I have called the new capitalism. As these enclaves contained capitalist entrepreneurs, so did they contain also a breed of intellectual not at all unlike those who surrounded the entrepreneurs and new men of power in France just before the French Revolution at the end of the eighteenth century. We are indebted to, first Burke, then Tocqueville, for noting the close relation that existed between the two groups, entrepreneurs and intellectuals, and for emphasizing their common hostility to the old order. If further explanation is needed for the affinity I speak of here, it can be found in some brilliant sections of Joseph Schumpeter's *Capitalism, Socialism, and Democracy.* There Schumpeter writes of the alienating effect of capitalism upon the very intellectuals it served to bring into existence as a class. Something of this was certainly to be seen in the university in the 1950s.

I am not disparaging the new breed of intellectual on the campus—the institute- and center-based breed—anymore than I am the generally radical cast of thought that this breed represented. In a sense, the political radicalism of many of this group was built into their rather ambiguous, marginal status on the campus. For all their undoubted academic ability, they lacked representation for the most part in the faculties, councils, and committees that formed the structure of academic government. True, the heads and certain other figures in the institutes and centers had this representation, for they served in the dual roles of professor and research entrepreneur. But in a fairly substantial number of other cases, such representation was lacking simply because the subordinate members of the research organizations, though possessed overwhelmingly of all necessary higher degrees, did not possess the professorial titles, in whatever grade, that were necessary to full membership on the faculty. As might be expected, a certain endemic restlessness or discontent was the consequence. And this could, of course, add to a set of mind that was already liberal to radical in disposition.

The new breed of intellectual in the academic centers and institutes which proliferated after the war was very different from the large number of technicians and scientists, mostly in the agriculture sector of the university, who had known for many years exactly the same lack of participation in academic government. Generally that group was either separated altogether from the campus—existing for the most part in experiment stations in the rural areas—or tradition was sufficient to restrain them. Something of the same was true immediately after the war in the great laboratories that physicists and chemists built and directed. They too had large, and on the whole politically quiescent, staffs of scientists and technicians who lacked representation. But as with the agriculturists these bodies tended to be physically separated from the heart of the university. And there is the well-known fact that physical scientists tend generally to be more conservative politically than humanists and social scientists. No such physical separation and no such political quiescence were to be found, however, in the ranks of the scholars and technicians who formed the staffs of the institutes and centers in the social sciences that multiplied during the late 1940s and the 1950s. Not perhaps a vital element in itself, the existence of this new breed of institute intellectual when added to other elements on the campus could, and did, lead to a quickening of the process of politicization.

There is no need to elaborate further. What I am writing about here is a matter of immediate memory for any who were on the campus in the 1950s. The national scene, the enormous increase in numbers of students and faculty members, the fracturing of the traditional structure of authority, the existence of more and more situations incapable of resolution through processes other than those of the adversary relationships of academic litigation, the rising number of blocs, caucuses, and similar groups, so suggestive of political parties, the ever more noticeable structuring of the faculty into persisting lefts, centers, and rights, with position on a given academic issue almost predictable when one knew what a given individual's "party" was, and the constantly proliferating issues of direct or derived political character—all of these were the signs of a politicization of the academic community that had never existed before; not, at least, in anything like the degree that had been reached by the middle 1950s.

And, as is always the case in societies undergoing severe social and economic change, administration tended to become ever more visible. Whereas up through World War II boards of trustees were themselves so inconspicuous as to suggest passion for anonymity, one became increasingly aware— again, mostly in public universities—of trustees, their individual identities, their ever lengthening meetings, their own constantly increasing numbers of committees, their ever more gala appearances on campuses, the ever greater amount of attention that they demanded from members of the university and from the media. Prior to about 1948 at Berkeley I very much doubt that members of the faculty, with rarest exceptions, even knew there was a Board of Regents. The great oath controversy changed that, of course. But even after pragmatic settlement of the oath controversy, the Regents of the University of California became much more visible on the campus and in the public generally.

Whereas, in earlier decades, appointment as a Regent was a quiet honor, one with no expectation of either public celebration or political power, such appointments became by the early 1950s political in character, with the "liberal" or "moderate" or "conservative" views of the individual not merely known but counted upon by the appointing governor. Whereas prior to about 1950 it was exceedingly rare for the governor (himself an *ex officio* Regent) to attend meetings of the Board of Regents and absolutely unheard of for such other political *ex officio* members of the board as the lieutenant-governor and the speaker of the Assembly to attend, meetings throughout the 1950s almost never were without these political figures present. There is simply no question but that the Board of Regents became a steadily more insistent more insistent and powerful political influence in the University of California during the decade.

The same was substantially true of administration generally in the University of California. It became steadily more visible, more active, more dominant, and more political— using that last word in the full sense. It also became steadily larger, both proportionately and absolutely. But never large enough. For once the processes of custom and of use and wont become replaced by the more formalized processes of litigation and direct administration, a new specialist has to be found for each of the multitudinous activities that are now to be found on a university campus. His very existence invites more duties, and more, and soon processes of binary fission have made him two, then four, then eight. Staffs and retinues of secretaries, technicians, clerks, specialists of all kinds enlarged constantly in the decade. (Not, however, noticeably where *student* interests and needs were concerned; the expansion was almost wholly in those areas that had been made imperious in demands by the new capitalism on the campus.)

And proliferation of formal administrators was accompanied in many places by almost identical proliferation of "nonadministrative" faculty committees. At Berkeley, for example, the number of academic senate committees was to double between 1945 and 1955. Meetings of the faculty became ever more formalized and bureaucratized (full-time staffs, presided over by full-time executive secretaries, themselves faculty members but relieved of all teaching and research duties) and ever more the objects of watchful concern by members of the different political blocs and parties on the campus. More and more faculty members could be heard saying (with what motives and what real feelings, no one could ever know for sure) that the hours spent in committee work far exceeded the hours spent in teaching and research.

I do not have to be told that Berkeley was, in most respects, unique until the latter part of the 1950s. So far as I know, no other major university in the country came very close to Berkeley in the extent and intensity of its politics: politics from the level of the Regents all the way down to politics at the student level. By comparison with a Berkeley, a Princeton or a Harvard was virtually lacking in the kind of politicization I am here referring to. One could spend a year on either of these campuses, or on the campus of any private university, and be scarcely aware of politics save as the muted thing that all academic novels have taken pains to try to make interesting to nonacademic readers, and without success. Unquestionably, special interests existed in these places, and these had to be dealt with more or less politically. Unquestionably, administrators, though relatively few, existed in these places, and they had to administer. Nevertheless, the most vivid impression that I—and many others during the 1940s and 1950s—acquired in visiting these places, even teaching in them, was the extraordinary difference in the extent and intensity of politics they manifested by comparison with what I knew intimately at Berkeley.

If I have emphasized Berkeley in so many places in this book it is not because I know it and its history so well. It is rather because events during recent years have proved repeatedly that Berkeley had been a kind of preview of what was to come in so many other universities in America in due time.

If Berkeley was the first major university (and it had become one of the world's really great universities by 1950, assessed by all the fundamental criteria) to know, in very large numbers, the new research entrepreneurs, the new men of power, and the new politics, it does not want for company at the present time.

The relation between impact of revolution on a social order and almost exponential increase in numbers of politicians and civil servants afterward is well known in the study of history. Berkeley has known three revolutions. The first, in 1919–1920, was a faculty insurrection—more accurately a kind of gentlemanly palace revolution involving only a small number of academically influential senior members of the faculty—whereby considerable delegation of powers was made directly by the Regents to the faculty, bypassing, in effect, the administration. Politically, Berkeley became a republic. The number of standing committees of the faculty, the number of express delegations of governing authority to these committees by the Regents, and the number of occasions on which politics, with its mustering of majorities, ruled, all of these were very considerable by the academic standards of the period 1920–1945. At Berkeley—and at other campuses of the University of California, all of which in substantial measure designed themselves along lines of Berkeley's academic senate—it was all regarded with pride, by most of the faculty at least. Rule by faculty instead of by administration—this, it was widely said at Berkeley, is the only way a university can be made great. If places such as Columbia, Princeton, and Harvard, none of which had anything like the amount of constant academic politics or the embedded distrust of administrators that was normal at Berkeley, listened to Berkeley's proud boasts with a certain amount of skeptical amusement, they can perhaps be forgiven. The newer nations have ever been more clamant in both their politics and the pride taken in politics.

The second revolution at Berkeley took place during 1949–1951 and was the consequence of the loyalty oath controversy during which the faculty resisted the efforts of certain Regents to impose upon all faculty members and employees of the University of California an oath whereby each person disclaimed and disavowed either belief or membership in subversive political organizations. The faculty won out—more or less [2]—but the consequences could have been

---

[2] Against the Regents-imposed oath, that is. It was, however, one of the "liberal" Regents, Governor Earl Warren, acting as governor in astute conjunction with Assemblyman Levering, who brought about

predicted by any informed reader of Tocqueville or Michels: far more intense politicization of the university generally and of the faculty specifically. Nothing like the political intensity of the faculty during the oath controversy had ever been seen before in any American university. Revolt became a part of the atmosphere. And this political intensity was to last throughout the 1950s at Berkeley. Predictably, the number of permanent faculty committees and councils shot up, and so did the number of politically tinged issues in the university. A permanent left and right were formed, with only the issues changing. There were times during the 1950s when one would have been justified in believing that the primary function of the faculty of the University of California, especially at Berkeley, was politics.

The effect of this constant atmosphere of politicization was, of course, to attract ever more politically-minded faculty members to the University of California. The iron doctrine of tenure assured a stable base from which to operate politically in any of a number of directions. Seemingly, it did not matter who was governor of the state, president of the university, chancellor or provost of a campus, dean of a school or college—that is, whether a "conservative" or a "liberal," a Democrat, a Republican, or a Socialist. The intensity of politicization of the faculty during the 1950s acquired a momentum of its own and increased constantly by a factor of its own.

Admittedly, the University of California was unique during the 1950s in the *visibility* of its politicization. But had any-

---

a state-imposed oath, mandatory on all public employees, including university faculty, that was far more rigorous and comprehensive than the Regents' oath.

one, watching the University of California from the ostensibly secure vantage point of a Harvard, Columbia, Michigan, or Wisconsin, chanced to murmur "It can't happen here," the answer could well have been: *De te fabula narratur.*

For, when the *third* revolution burst forth at Berkeley in 1964, the so-called student revolution, the opening shot was to be heard 'round the academic world. All that had been present in fact but largely invisible to naked eye at these universities, and a great many others, suddenly surfaced in the single greatest crisis that has ever been experienced by the American university.

❧ 11 ❧

THE STUDENT REVOLUTION

THE STUDENT UPRISINGS which began at Berkeley in 1964 did not destroy academic authority. It was the prior destruction of academic authority that in very large measure caused the student uprisings.

In his epochal study of the French Revolution, written a half-century after the event, Tocqueville wrote: "Chance played no part whatever in the outbreak of the Revolution: though it took the world by surprise, it was the inevitable outcome of a long period of gestation, the abrupt and violent conclusion of a process in which six generations had played intermittent part. Even if it had not taken place, the old social structure would nonetheless have been shattered everywhere sooner or later." [1]

Much the same can be said about the student insurrections which began at Berkeley in 1964 and still have no easily foreseeable ending. In retrospect it is plain that the specific reasons given by the earliest student insurrectionaries—Viet

[1] Alexis de Tocqueville, *The Old Regime and the Revolution* (New York: Doubleday and Company, Anchor Books, 1955), p. 20.

Nam, black civil rights, corruption of the middle class, and so on—only partly explain the pattern of the uprisings. Given the condition of academic authority and of the academic community by the end of the 1950s, after a decade and a half of the economic, social, intellectual, and political changes we have been considering, one is justified in asking today: How could some kind of revolution *not* have begun?

Bear in mind that none of the student insurrections, at least in such major centers as Berkeley, Harvard, Columbia, Michigan, and Wisconsin, were motivated by concern with *academic* matters. Since there has been so much misunderstanding on this point, especially in the media, I shall come back to it in the final paragraphs of this chapter. But even if these uprisings were stimulated by extramural issues, we are left with the problem of why the university campus, rather than some other part of the social order, should have been the base of revolutionary forays and, most important, should have proved itself pathetically incapable from the very beginning of dealing with the student uprisings.

In short, no matter what specific goals were offered by the student revolutionists at Berkeley in 1964, and then in dozens of other places during the ensuing years, the vital question remains: how could the revolutions have begun *in the university,* the one institution that prior to World War II, at least, could claim the greatest dedication among all institutions to humane reason and progressive liberalism? And, having begun in one of the greatest, most liberal, democratic, and emancipated of universities, Berkeley, how could the insurrections have managed to go on as long as they have? Although in large degree these questions have been answered in the foregoing chapters, it will be clarifying to consider the student revolution now, not only against the background of the changes and dislocations we have considered but, more to the point here, against the well-substantiated knowledge we have of how revolutions take place generally.

We must make no mistake about the reality of revolutionary tides in our day. Although a revolution against the American social order in any large-scale, much less successful, sense is as unlikely—short of some prior cataclysmic disabling of American political power—as anything one might think of, the fact remains: a revolution, or at least a series of profoundly crippling insurrections, in the American university is one of the central facts in the history of the second half of the twentieth century. We may dismiss as vagaries of political romanticism the declarations by student leaders, from Mario Savio, Mark Rudd, and Jerry Rubin onward, of revolutionary war against American society. But we cannot dismiss the extent to which the insurrectionaries have been able to dominate the affairs of certain American universities for nearly a decade; nor can we dismiss idly the impact such insurrections will surely have for a long time upon academic policy in this country and upon popular support from the citizenry.

In other words, at least within the confines of the university in America something approximating a revolution has taken place. What I want to do in this chapter is put this revolution, or rather its effective causes and conditions, in the context of what we know about the outbreaks of revolutions in other places and at other times. I shall be brief, limiting myself to the essential points that have emerged from the comparative study of revolutions.

The preliminary condition of our understanding of any revolution, political, economic, or academic, is abandonment of the mystique of the masses, of the kind of political romanticism that sees revolutions in the image of the volcano, with long pent-up, widespread, and passionate mass demands suddenly erupting. The official histories of most revolutions, including the American Revolution at the end of the eighteenth century, have been written substantially in these terms. Whether the American, the French, or the Russian Revolution, our conventional understanding tends to run toward the familiar picture of revolutionary *masses*. So too with the student insurrections of the past decade. For a number of years, despite the relatively small number of insurrectionists, despite their own utterly clear statements of why they were rebelling, the media in this country could not be disabused of the more romantic notion that the revolts at Berkeley, San Francisco State, Harvard, Columbia, and elsewhere were in fact *mass* revolts of students, the volcanic release of many years of student demands left unmet in matters of curriculum and teaching.[2]

But as every careful study of the student uprisings has shown clearly enough, the overwhelming majority of students ranged from indifference to hostility in their attitude toward the uprisings. There may have been, there was, a certain degree of resentment, of alienation, even of bitterness toward the university and toward what this majority could sense, if not altogether understand, about what I have called the higher capitalism and that whole restructuring of

[2] Alas, if only the student insurrectionaries *had* been, in any substantial degree, genuinely concerned with curriculum, teaching, academic honor, authority, and community! One could be more optimistic about the future of the university in America.

the postwar university that destroyed academic community. But to find revolutionary potential in this feeling of the great majority is absurd. So, as such students of comparative revolution as Tocqueville, Michels, Mosca, Taine, Peter Drucker, and Hannah Arendt have made vivid to us, is it absurd to find revolutionary potential in the masses anywhere, anytime. The existence of disaffected, alienated, atomized masses may make revolutions possible at certain times in history. But masses do not themselves create revolutions, no matter how widespread conditions such as poverty, inequity, injustice, and alienation may be among them. The existence of a large number of students for whom the American university had become an alien structure assuredly set the scene in which the student insurrectionaries could operate so successfully. But that is all.

What, then, are the conditions of revolution generally and, specifically of the student revolution of the past decade? I offer the following.

First, there must be a preceding period of sharp, almost convulsive change in society, especially in the economic and social spheres. Change is never a pleasant experience for any people, not even those who might objectively be thought to be drawing benefits from it. Change, when it is substantial, affects not merely codes of authority, customs, and established ways of doing things: it enters into social roles and statuses. Change cannot help but create a specter of uncertainty that hovers over people, making recourse to power seem sometimes not only salutary but redemptive. Change, then, of established social functions, of social authorities, and of social roles—in at least a significant minority of a population—is the prime condition of revolution. The American colonies, France, Russia, all of these knew very substantial change, chiefly economic, during the decades immediately preceding their revolutions. So, as we have seen, did the American campus during the two decades leading up to 1960.

Second, there must be a strong feeling of the breakdown of established authority; or, if not breakdown, at least of confusion of authority. Legitimacy of old authority must be in some doubt, at least in the minds of a determining minority of the people. There must be a mounting degree of ill-resolved conflict of authority, with new centers of authority —based on new centers of wealth—in, but not wholly in, the network of total authority. Competition, even hostile rivalry, between old centers and the new ones in the larger structure of authority must exist.

Third, there must be a considerable degree of affluence. Despite the folklore of revolution, peoples plunged in deep poverty do not revolt. Only those who are emerging fairly rapidly from poverty—or at least large sections emerging rapidly—are likely to countenance revolt for any significant period of time. There must be enough feel of possessions, enough sense of affluence, to make the sense of what *hasn't* been achieved a galling one. It is *relative* deprivation, not absolute deprivation, that is the key here. Again, as is well known, France in the eighteenth century, Russia in the early twentieth century, the American university campus in the mid-twentieth century, were all settings of very considerable affluence for at least a great many. But by the same token, they were settings of increasingly strong feelings of relative deprivation. Affluence never spreads itself equally through a society. It did not in the university of the 1950s. Always there were groups that could be thought better off, unjustly better off, than one's own. The "old" faculty had never had it so good in terms of salaries, teaching loads, offices, and research assistance. But comparison with the "new" faculty, masters of institutes, centers, and bureaus, holders of vast contractual grants, who exhibited a life style that seemed somehow foreign to the nature of the university in the judgments of the "old" faculty, made tensions inevitable. And these tensions conveyed themselves to students.

Fourth, there must be a substantial measure of liberalization achieved during the period before the revolution. Here again folklore has it that revolutions break out among peoples deeply oppressed. Peoples may *feel* themselves opressed, or minorities may, but invariably we find that marked liberalizations of life have taken place: in political and legal as well as customary terms. It is the liberalization of the old regime that makes possible, at one and the same time, the feeling of relative deprivation of freedom and the means of doing something about it. The people of France, of Russia, and students in the universities were politically freer during the years just preceding revolution than they ever had been before. When one thinks of the restrictions on faculty and student life—on the campus, at any rate—prior to World War II, the conditions after the war were close to utopia for all those desiring political freedom on the campus. But it wasn't utopian enough. And, happily, opportunities to make it more utopian lay all about. These were seized on in rising degree between 1958 and 1964. All over the country a wave of student-participating, though wholly peaceful, liberalization of restrictions on nonacademic existence could be seen. It crested about 1964.

Fifth, there must be a striking politicization already going on. This is important, for even though such politicization is largely of the administrative type, the uses of power are made resplendent. It is a matter of record that established political bodies are in ever more feverish condition in the decades prior to a revolution: numbers of meetings go up, lengths of meetings become greater, and the business of the meetings becomes ever more swollen. Political bodies also become more visible to the public eye; characteristically, there is greater ostentation about these bodies. Most important, however, as many matters as possible that were previously in the realm of mere custom or use and wont must be transferred to the more rationalized, more formalized, more adversary-prone, capacities of the political system. More and more matters become seized, then, by politics and by hope of achievement of goals through political means.

Sixth, there must be power-sensitive, power-eager, intellectual elites. Intellectuals as a political class came into being in substantial numbers in the eighteenth century, and it is no accident that Paris was nearly overrun with them. The *philosophes* set the pattern: keen minds, brilliantly informed rather than profound, activity-driven, able to move like lions in the salons of the rich and powerful, basically rootless, and obsessed by the capture of power—not for themselves to wield directly but to dominate those wielding it. It is not necessary for members of these elites to be themselves oriented toward any single thrust of a nation or large organization. Elites may, and usually do, contain novelists, poets, and scientists, as well as those directly interested in the study of human behavior. Disagreements and hostilities among themselves are often great, with factions and cliques the consequence. But, no matter how divided, all alike tend to see the world in political terms and to crave power.

Seventh, there must be some precipitating incident or event, one that, while in no way necessarily related to internal conditions, succeeds in bringing passions to ever greater boil and, with this, potential mobilization of numbers. The incident may be something like the Boston massacre, the storming of the Bastille, the firing upon the assembly before the Winter Palace. It may as large in scope as the impact of World War I on the Russian masses. Or it may be as small, relatively speaking, as the arrest of two or three insurrectionists or rioters by the police on a campus. It does not matter what or how large the precipitating incident is. But such an incident is vital: otherwise there is no means of lighting the spark necessary to revolutionary fire.

Eighth, the moral issues must be made somehow appealing to substantial numbers. The atmosphere of idealism, however bogus it may be in terms of underlying realities, must form, giving blanket to the inevitable harshnesses, the inescapable violence, the occasional atrocity of revolutionary behavior. The roots of idealism, of moralism, may lie in the philosophical works of a Rousseau or Voltaire; in the pamphlets of a John Hancock or Tom Paine; in the manifestoes of a working-class movement. Or, as was the case in America in the early 1960s, in the oftentimes courageous acts of militant students seeking an end to the war in Viet Nam or to discrimination against blacks. Had it not been for the cast of idealism formed very early at Berkeley, a cast that could soon encompass issues, academic included, that in the beginning had been utterly alien to the militants' zeal, the insurrections there would not have lasted very long. But the image of the idealistic student, struggling for recognition in a hostile, bureaucratic, indifferent university proved to be a powerful image; one that—in the media, in much of the public mind for two or three years, in the faculty, in the board of trustees, and elsewhere—served the militants well all the while their eyes were fixed on targets very different from the university curriculum. Irrespective of the actual causes of a revolution, the actual objectives, be these working-class, socialist, or fascist, and the actual day-to-day motivations, idealism and moralism are indispensable as atmosphere.

Ninth, it must be easy to contrast an existing scene of declared corruption, hypocrisy, and insensitivity to human rights with a utopia summoned up either from the romanticized past, some primordial Garden, or from the imaginary future. It is always difficult, nay, impossible, to deny the existence of corruption and hypocrisy in some degree at least around one; such is the human condition. But how does one say this valorously or nobly at a time when militant idealism, real or bogus, is holding up the allure of a world in which neither corruption, nor hypocrisy, nor any other vice, can exist? In the beginning the student revolutionists were in no way interested in the structure of the American university. And even later their claimed interest in curriculum and academic policy had a rather hollow ring alongside their manifestly transcending, ostentatiously millennial interest in, first national, then world revolution. But the support that student militants received for two or three years at least from press, faculty, and a surprisingly large sector of the public came from the skill with which their leaders taunted faculty and administration with the all-too-visible marks of what I have called in this book academic capitalism, managerialism, and of endemic faculty politicization.

We have the word—written as well as oral—of all the major student revolutionaries, from Mario Savio to Mark Rudd, that the condition of the university mattered little to them save as one more illustration of a social order that was in their view irredeemably corrupt and obsolete. Whatever else these militants may have been, they did not lack a certain forthrightness, even honesty, about long-range goals. But they would have been very stupid indeed if they had not seized upon issues that were, in effect, handed to them by press, faculty, and administration.

Tenth, there must be a certain reservoir of guilt in the Establishment of a social order or institution if revolt is to be gotten off to a good start. There are enough memoirs and diaries available to make us aware of the dimensions of guilt that in time came to seize the minds of aristocrats in Paris, later in St. Petersburg, and still later in the ruling councils of the American university. As I indicated in the chapter on the cult of individuality, much of the so-called experimentalism that took place in curriculum during the late 1940s and throughout the 1950s was a means of expiating for the vague sense of guilt that went with the higher capitalism and the whole affluent, large-scale research-oriented world of the student-avoiding, teaching-repulsing, and community-disdaining new men of power. It will suffice here to say that the reservoir of faculty, administrative, and alumni guilt had become rather substantial by 1964. The light and leading of the academic world may not have been aware of it prior to the autumn of 1964. But once the student insurrections began, the sense of guilt hung over the academic landscape in

America just as it had over the minds of aristocrats in Paris and in St. Petersburg earlier.

These, then, are the crucial characteristics of any revolution. Slogans, announced goals, ideals, and objectives are as varied as history itself. Nor do I say these are unimportant; not at all. But they are not crucial. In retrospect it is possible to see that even had there been no issues of Viet Nam, of black civil rights, or of polluted environment, revolution or insurrection in some form would have taken place at Berkeley—and then spread to the rest of the academic world. The accumulated results of nearly two decades of the higher capitalism, managerialism, and Faustian humanitarianism, as well as the broken structure of academic community resulting from these and other forces, would have seen to that. Once more I am obliged to repeat: the student militants were not concerned with any of these at any point, except as they might have now and then provided popular justification for their existence. With a whole society, even world, to be saved, how could one have expected other than passing interest in such trivial matters as teaching, counseling, and study? With a vast millennial community of mankind to be achieved, how could one care about that tiny part of the social bond known as the academic community?

Nevertheless, had it not been for the accumulated results of all the powerful changes that affected the American university from 1945 on, the student revolution could not have gotten started. Even had it gotten started, it could never have survived its first week; anymore than any such revolution could have commenced, or been long sustained, during the 1930s.

PART III

The Future of
the Academic Dogma

There are no revolutions that do not shake existing belief, enervate authority, and throw doubts
over commonly received ideas. Every revolution
has more or less the effect of releasing men to
their own conduct and of opening before the mind
of each one of them an almost limitless perspective. . . . Everyone then attempts to be his own
sufficient guide and makes it his boast to form his
own opinions on all subjects. Men are no longer
bound together by ideas, but by interests; and it
would seem as if human opinions were reduced to
a sort of intellectual dust, scattered on every side,
unable to collect, unable to cohere.

ALEXIS DE TOCQUEVILLE,
Democracy in America, vol. 2, ch. 1

12

THE SEARCH FOR
ACADEMIC COMMUNITY

Many and varied are the proposals today for the rejuvenation of the university. At every hand the premise of moribundity in the historic and traditional university serves as the base for some projection in which the university is seen as taking on new mission, new function, and regained strength. Nearly all of these projections or proposals, it is worth noting at the outset, are themselves drawn from the revolutionary changes in the university during the past quarter-century. Each of these changes becomes an image, as it were, of the university of the future. There is a strong tendency, in short, to look into the future and see only a magnification of some present and recently gained attribute of the heterogeneous academic society to which Clark Kerr has given the name "multiversity."

In this chapter I shall consider briefly a few of the more prominent projections of the university into the future, offering in each instance the criticisms that seem to me most pertinent.

1

The university as capstone of the research establishment. This view is a tempting one, given "realism" by the ascendant position of the university in large-scale research and "idealism" by society's manifest need for knowledge. It is said that the university's last great hope lies in assuming dominance of the sciences and technology. Hence the imperative necessity of carrying the university even further into the realm of institutes and centers, with their full-time devotion to high-level, large-scale research. Only thus, it is said, can our technological society be maintained; and only thus can our universities continue to receive the support from government, industry, and foundation that is vital to preservation of the university in the foreseeable future.

This conception of the future university is inevitably an appealing one to all those whose lives currently fall within the higher academic capitalism. To see the university as one vast research institute, with all else made subsidiary or superfluous, and with this vast research institute serving as the highest level of the national research establishment, does have a substantial attraction for more than a few within the university's walls.

But I am afraid I cannot see this conception having very much appeal in the long run to those who will bear the economic costs: the federal government, state governments, industry, and the foundations. The reason can be stated simply. The expense would be astronomical. Large-scale research today in the sciences is expensive enough under the best of circumstances. Even in organizations which have been designed meticulously for the express purpose of high-level research the costs are extremely high. Why, then, put the research in a setting—the university—that cannot, by its very organizational nature, avoid multiplying these costs?

I assume that those who see the university as the capstone of the national research establishment have in mind, when they refer to the university, something at least roughly comparable to what now exists, even to what has traditionally existed, allowing only for the dislocating changes I described in the preceding section. This means an institution in which at least some teaching continues, in which presumably the humanities and arts and social sciences, as well as physical and biological sciences, would exist, and in which—given the existence of students—a plethora of other activities, some curricular, some noncurricular, would go on.

All of these are, however, expensive economically, and they cannot help distracting the managers and workers in the great laboratories, institutes, and centers that would carry the brunt of research responsibility under the envisagement I am describing here. Even assuming, as we are obliged to assume, an imminent end to the kinds of interference with government- and industry-sponsored research on the campus that have characterized the past decade of the student revolution on the campus, there would remain a large number of styles of behavior, thought, and action which, however desirable when assessed by traditional academic criteria, would be both disruptive and costly to a bona fide research establishment.

The point is that the university in any recognizable form is very far from being a "rational" and "economic" organization. It was never intended to be when its internal structures of faculties, colleges, and schools, its roles of provost, dean, professor, and student, and its guild-like, quasi-aristocratic organization came into being. I do not say that these qualities are inimical to research and scholarship. Far from it. As we have seen, the university, in contrast to the college, is built on the pillar of research as much as upon teaching. *But the kind of research that is compatible with teaching!* From the point of view of teaching-in-research and research-in-teaching the inherited structure of the university makes some sense. From the point of view of highly rationalized, bureaucratized, large-scale research alone, however, the inherited structure makes very little sense. If it be said that it was to the universities that the government and industry were forced to turn a generation ago when science at highest level was needed for military and other national research problems, the answer is: they no longer are so forced.

The reason is the mushrooming of governmental, industrial, and foundation-sponsored centers of research in America that are becoming ever more attractive both to sponsoring agencies and to more than a few scientists still holding, for one reason or other, to university jobs. Such centers need only to be developed and multiplied, through proper contracts with sponsoring agencies, for them to assume just about all large-scale research responsibilities in our society. They will be far more rational to the end in view, certainly less expensive, than are, or ever could be, institutes within academic walls that are forced to make terms with the demands of the traditional university. For these, however isolated they may be, relatively speaking, from the normal activities of the university at the present time, however much they may look like fastnesses of industrial-govern-mental enterprise within the academy, do have to make *some* concessions to the guild that contains them.

And I do not doubt that a substantial number of scientists now in the university, those at least whose work is of the large-scale, rarefied kind that depends upon expensive equip-ment and upon insulation from the customary hurly-burly of the university and its ordinary activities, would find the transfer from university to nonacademic research center a highly gratifying one. For a long time the elbowroom, the intellectual autonomy, and the sheer status of being at a Berkeley, Columbia, or Michigan was sufficient to hold such individuals to the university, to prevent them from going to government and industry. Now, however, that the prestige of the university is fast-diminishing in our society and that nonacademic institutes have learned the valuable lesson of giving privacy and elbowroom to their members in their research, the traditional ties to the university are beginning to dissolve.

From the strictly economic and rational point of view the time is past, alas, when the salary of the Chaucerian scholar must be made to match, or at least be within range of, the salary of the physicist or biologist. Such equity is and has been the genius of the university. Within its community and under its dogma all scholars and teachers have the same value. Which is proper when they are assessed by the criteria of the traditional university or by the criteria of humane thought. But they do *not* have the same value when assessed, as a vast amount of research in the university today has to be assessed, by the criteria of national need, of military or political priority, and of the market place generally.

Once the higher capitalism was brought into the university

by those scientists and scholars whose "productivity" was marketable to government and industry, the criteria of success changed radically, as we have seen. To suppose that scientists with potentially high earning capacity are going to enjoy subsidizing, in effect, their colleagues who lack this capacity in the market place, who are, so to speak, lilies of the field, is to supose nonsense. When I say "subsidize" I speak advisedly. There is only one reason why, since World War II, salaries of classicists, historians, philologists, philosophers, and a great many others in the humanities and social sciences have for the most part kept pace with the salaries of the natural scientists: *the academic dogma!*

Add to this the prestige that even the greatest of the scientists took on by being at a Harvard or Berkeley or Chicago instead of, say, Rand or some other research institute. Scientists fully able to command large salaries in the market place were perfectly willing to see the salaries of the Chaucerian scholar and other humanists rise along with their own. Such was the prestige of the university. Events of the past decade have, however, radically altered that perspective. One may confidently expect the number and the attractiveness of non-academic research centers to rise markedly in the years immediately ahead, and one may with equal confidence expect to see scientists move in swelling numbers from the universities to these centers.

On some dread day—so might run the nightmare today of any university president committed to the higher academic capitalism—all congressional committees, industrial boards of directors, and foundation executives will realize at once that there are far cheaper and more efficient places to have their research done than in the academic guild that is the university. And, at the same time, all physicists, chemists, mathematicians, biologists, and engineers, the ones, that is, that universities like to hold, will realize that by going to these new kinds of research center or institute they can have higher salaries for not having to share them with the Chaucerian scholar, freedom from the now-augmenting distractions of university existence, and, if things keep going the way they are, much higher status in the American social system.

The above paragraph is no doubt speculative. What is not speculative is the demonstrable fact that the inherently great expense of large-scale research today is vastly increased by having it done in an organization in any way comparable to the traditional university.

I happen to think that the higher capitalism, glittering as its wealth seemed just after World War II to countless trustees and university administrators, has proved a bad bargain for the universities themselves. I mean *economically,* for the fact of the bad bargain sociologically, spiritually, and academically has been, I think, sufficiently demonstrated in this book. It has been an economically bad bargain for the university in America for the reason that no matter how large the "override" (it approaches 30 percent at the present time in many universities), the amount gained is still insufficient to cover the real costs that have attended the presence of the resplendent structures of the higher capitalism on the campus. There is a lovely illusion that sees support for the humanities and all the noble things in life as benign byproducts of the Pentagon contracts with scientists on the campus. But it is only that: an illusion. Someday, when people skilled in the analysis of university budgets, of *real* costs measured in terms of rising expectations, architectural magnificence, affluent style of life, and so forth, make their long-needed report on the financial realities of the quarter-century following World War II in the American university, the illusion finally will be punctured forever. As I said in an earlier chapter: the first million dollars accruing to universities under the higher capitalism were far too much. Today ten billion dollars are not enough.

But even if I am wrong about the financial damage done the universities, there is simply no question of my other and essential point. From any rational, strictly economic point of view at the present time, the great funding agencies, starting with the federal government, are doubling, at very least, their costs in having their research done within the Middle Ages-sprung university. Unlike the situation existing a generation ago, there are, at the present time, very attractive alternatives, and one would be foolish to suppose these alternatives will not suggest themselves to the funding agencies.

In sum, the rather odd structure that is the university makes an admirable setting for what it and its roles were designed for: teaching-in-research and research-in-teaching; or, if we prefer, the kind of research that is inseparable from classroom and seminar. It is grotesquely unsuited for being capstone of the national research establishment.

2

The university as the microcosm of culture. In the realm of "high culture" this envisagement has much in common with the preceding one. Instead of the scientist and technologist making the university the scene of their full-time creative work, we may think instead of the artist: the novelist, poet, painter, musician, sculptor, all of whom, from the time art became an autonomous activity in human society, have required some form of patronage. Since the Church does not easily come to mind as patron today, nor aristocracy either, why not the university? The campus would become the scene of resident artists in every field—analogous, as I have just suggested, to resident scientists and resident technologists.

It is an appealing idea. Let us pass quickly over the economic difficulty. Granted that most taxpayers would probably balk in due time, they might not; they might become as thoroughly art-conscious as presumably the Athenians of the fifth century B.C. were. Let us, in any event, assume that there would be no substantial economic objection.

The *social* difficulty seems to me insuperable in the long run. I do not suggest that no artist can live happily and work creatively on the campus. Quite a number do. But generally speaking the rather corporate and curricular atmosphere of the university does not serve the artist well. Granted that stable income and tenure would be welcome, perhaps irresistible to the individual artist. And I do not pretend to know exactly what the proper circumstances are for the nourishing of first-rate art—literary, musical, or whatever—beyond having a profound sense that the greatest ages in the arts we have record of did not incorporate their artists in organizations like the university. The nearest exception is the Middle Ages. Beyond doubt most artists were then working in guilds or within the rather tight structure of the Church. But even the medieval period had its full share of Villons, of composers of poetry, of ballad, and of epic, as well as of performers wandering about the country for whom the guild, the corporation—lay or ecclesiastical—was not desirable. And it is somehow hard to imagine the greatest of our sagas, epics, novels, poems, paintings, quartets, and symphonies having been done by tenured professors solemnly attending faculty meetings every month and meeting classes every day on schedule. I am not implying that artists like economic or any other type of insecurity; or that they work without discipline; far from it. I am suggesting, however, that between the best of art and the university or guild there may be something of the incompatibility of temperament that one finds between guild and individual entrepreneur. It is highly probable that even where art does thrive in relatively communal atmosphere, such atmosphere would have to be rather different from that of the university.

One is not, I think, indulging in the romantic fallacy about the artist when he suggests that the artist requires a substantially greater individual freedom from restraints of time and place and also a greater, more varied field of experience to draw from than the university can easily supply. Basically I think it as wrong to suppose that the artist is helped by the university atmosphere as it is to suppose that the prophet or rebel is helped appreciably. Each may draw something from what is native to the university, but none will draw very much that is contributory to his larger role.

The university is not for everyone—not even, and especially, for the brilliantly and creatively endowed mind—in all areas. Here too we run into that fallacy, drawn from deep respect for the university in the social order, which says, in effect, there must be something to appeal to all, to the most diversely constituted, in the university. It must be all things. But it cannot be and it destroys itself in trying to be. Several times I have made the distinction in this book between the two traditions of knowledge, one requiring, being inseparable from, scholarship and the communal atmosphere of teaching and learning; the other not requiring this, being indeed profoundly limited by it. One may, I think, place the artist, whether writer, composer, or performer, much nearer the latter. He may not be actually spoiled by the academic atmosphere. But there is no evidence I am aware of that he is helped by it in the creative sense, and the evidence is surely clear that the Shakespeares, Mozarts, Cezannes, and Dostoevskys in history, including the Joyces, Prousts, Eliots, Yeats, and Stravinskys of our own day, have been rather far from the kind of tradition and atmosphere the university excels in.

3

The university as adjunct to Establishment. This conception of the university can ground itself, I suppose, in the Greek ideal of philosopher-king. But translated into modern political and administrative realities, it has as little feasibility as does either of the other two envisagements of the university.

Not that it is without foundation in present actuality. Just as most of the greater university campuses these days have their resident technologists and resident artists, so they have their resident politicians or, if we prefer, resident advisers to the President or to governors, to Congress or the Cabinet, to civil or foreign service. And, conversely, many a full-time government administrator has in recent years spent a kind of retreat on the campus. Under this view, the university would provide academic respite for short periods to the administrator, industrial manager, labor leader; and the areas of government, industry, and labor from which these individuals came would also house for short periods the professors drawn from disciplines relevant to them. The university under this conception would be a kind of clearinghouse for theory and practice, for teaching and administration of government and industry, and for all the other activities flowing from the effort to make the university a reflecting glass of the vast world of administration.

I am afraid I do not see this conception proving very useful or attractive to either side—university professors or governmental and other administrators. There is the rare individual—the Daniel P. Moynihan, the Henry Kissinger—who can seemingly move without great effort from scholarship and teaching to distinguished work in high governmental office. There are not many such individuals.

By nature the university scholar, even the university administrator, whether of institute and bureau or of the more traditional types of organization in the university, is not used to the sweat of politics, the odor of expediency, the clutch of compromise. The academic man especially—say, a political scientist or sociologist or economist—finds it hard to conquer certain feelings of distaste for the representative from Iowa, the senator from Mississippi or California, and most of the tens of thousands of civil servants. Our academic man's distaste shows. You can take the professor out of the campus but such is the persisting influence of the academic dogma even these days—you can't take the campus out of the professor. This, on the evidence of much testimony and many memoirs, is the fatal flaw in the conception of the university as a kind of administrative bank, always ready to lend its light and leading to governments for high internal or foreign assignments.

Everything that has made an individual a distinguished scholar (and who ever heard of a distinguished *teacher* being selected to serve as head of a major agency in Washington or as ambassador) tends to unfit him for the job of living with decisions that must be made immediately. No matter how valuable, invaluable indeed, the scholar's study of a given subject may be, that is, his book or monograph on the subject, when it comes to direct advice *now,* there is usually a certain crippling tenuosity about his recommendations made directly to the situation. To the agonized superior's What Do We Do? the academic man can usually answer only in terms of models, value assumptions, what-has-been-done-that-shouldn't-have-been-done, and extrapolations of trends considered in light of further models and assumptions, and so on. Principle invariably prospers in such circumstances; government tends to, if not perish, go dry. The academic dogma has prepared its disciples for the long run. Sweaty, political, interest-ridden, crisis-impending government lives, alas, in the short run.

The difficulty works in reverse direction. The university considered as governmental and industrial clearinghouse is usually no better off for the presence of major figures from these areas on the campus than the government bureau is for the presence of the professor on leave. How often has one witnessed the discomfort of the distinguished industrialist, labor leader, or government official when, instead of the lecture or colloquium that is often stimulating and first-rate intellectually, he has been persuaded to spend a whole term or year on the campus. He is bored, nothing in his own role fits him for easy occupancy of the professional role, and above all he must teach. Teaching is an art form. It can be done brilliantly or appallingly. But teaching, in class, meeting by meeting, over an extended period, is as much an art form as a three-act play. Hence the acute agony of a genuinely knowledgeable, even profound and erudite individual who has been accustomed to administering, or even writing books and plays, when the responsibility for a course is placed on him.

It would be nice to think that the secretary of state could automatically give a good course. Or any of the several top, permanent, persons in the Department. But they almost never can. They have accumulated a great deal of knowledge, but they have never accumulated the techniques and playings of role that go into teaching as an art form. It is not at all unlike the individual with a superb plot in mind for a play who has not the remotest sense of sequences of acts and scenes. Trustees sometimes think they are doing conservatism and the business establishment some good when they manage to get professorships set up on a rotating basis for businessmen, professionals, and others "out in the real world." In fact they tend, by so doing, to set conservatism and the appeal of business to the undergraduate badly back. Even the politically liberal economist, bona fide academic economist, who knows how to conduct a course, does more for the business world than does, say, the president of a great corporation who stumbles and fumbles through a term-length course.

I am not suggesting here total segregation of the university from the business-labor-religious-governmental areas of administration any more than in the other instances we have considered. There are various modes of interaction that are effective. But any thought of the university cast permanently and largely in these terms makes very little sense.

4

The university as radical critic of society. Beyond doubt, there are many in the universities these days who proudly identify themselves as *radical* psychologists, political scientists, sociologists, and even biologists and chemists, though in diminishing numbers in these areas of huge research budgets. And a few of them have very recently publicly declared this to be the soundest role for the university in the future: to be radical, to serve as revolutionary conscience and, at the same time, goad. It too is an appealing prospect. Every society needs such a conscience and goad. Societies without them are characteristically lethargic and intellectually immobile even if, as the historical evidence shows, such societies do go on surviving for millennia.

The chief question, however, is simply the fitness of the academic for the undoubtedly valuable role of revolutionist-to-the-Establishment. It is not so much that Establishments don't like paid, tenured, privileged revolutionists in their service, for the testimony of many Establishments in history is that their members, or many of them, do indeed enjoy such revolutionists around. The French aristocracy, as we know, rather liked the *philosophes;* certainly liked them at the gatherings in their salons, just as the Kennedy administration liked them at its White House parties and on its rolling Virginia estates. No, this is not the problem. The problem is the capacity of the academic to *be* a revolutionist. He almost never has in history. One can *call* himself, even when he is not a full professor with iron tenure, a radical political scientist, and beyond a doubt, by the political scientists he is a radical. But by the *radicals* what is he? Ay, that is the question!

Alas, the testimony of most of the radicals in modern European history—the *philosophes,* Bentham, Proudhon, Marx, Sorel et al.—is that he is no radical; only an academic, culling from one ancient Western tradition of thought instead of some other. What the Mario Savios, Jerry Rubins, and Mark Rudds had to discover painfully in the 1960s for themselves was already a matter of record in some of the utterances of their early predecessors: that in the academic, no matter what he may call himself, too much of the academic dogma lingers, giving him the pale cast of thought, of austere piety, but rarely the juices of action. The evidence remains today what the evidence has been for a long time in the West. If one desires radicalism he will go where the radicals are, not to departments of political science and sociology in the affluent universities.[1]

Anyhow, radicalism, if it is to rise above the level of rhetorical piety, must be associated in some way with a mass movement. Marx, Proudhon, and Sorel all knew this. So did Lenin. So do Mao, Castro, and others know it. Academics do not, however, seem to mingle much more successfully with the toiling or disadvantaged masses than they do with the sweating politicians and the bureaucracy-bound civil servants in Washington. Academics have, by virtue of whatever of the academic dogma has rubbed off on them, trained incapacities in all these areas.

Imagine the radical political scientist or sociologist—that is, if he is indeed a political scientist or sociologist, and not just a hanger-on—surviving very long the trials and torments,

---

[1] Historically, the mark of the rebel, the radical revolutionist, has been willingness to put possessions, security, and status behind him. Not since the loyalty-oath battle at Berkeley two decades ago have I heard of an academic radical willing to put so much as his second car behind him. If conservatism tends to have rural roots and authentic radicalism urban roots, those of the faculty radical are surely suburban.

and especially the simple civilities, of revolutionary fellow-
ship. Academics tend for the most part to be so accustomed
to the deference of graduate students, the cap-touching respect of younger colleagues hoping for promotion, and the
genuflections of administrators' wives that the ordinary demands of revolutionary action would shortly prove desolating.
For, let us not forget, there is nothing very democratic about
the academic dogma. Born of quasi-aristocratic circumstances, it has maintained itself all these centuries by, not
revolutionary or even working-class association, but by the
constraints and buffers, including hierarchy and tenure, of the
academically aristocratic community.

This is obviously not to say that a member of the academic
community cannot have a radical *mind*. McIlwain's *High
Court of Parliament,* Schumpeter's *Capitalism, Socialism,
and Democracy,* and, very recently, Edward Banfield's *The
Unheavenly City* are all radical books in the sense that each
has dared to break with conventional understandings, and in
ways that, history tells us, can have very radical consequences. Adam Smith's *The Wealth of Nations* was a radical
book. We need look only at its profound impact upon Parliamentary legislation, among other places in the nineteenth
century, to be assured of this. Karl Marx's *Capital* was a
radical book and has very clearly had long-run radical consequences. Neither it, nor any of the others I have mentioned,
is, however, other than a piece of profound scholarship that
dared to break with conventional understandings.

But all of this is a far cry from the conception of radicalism that seems to activate the self-styled radical social scientist at the present, whose idea of the university's serving as
radical conscience of society is, as a first step, to scuttle

scholarship and adopt the posture of permanent attack upon
the Establishment, academic and other. As I say, nothing in
the professorial role fits him in any way for radicalism in this
sense of the word. Nor should it.

5

The university as humanitarian-in-chief. Again, I want to
emphasize that far from any disdain for humanitarian enterprise as such, either inside or outside the university, I honor
it. And within limits there is no reason why the university
should not be engaged in direct humanitarian service, just as
is state, church, industry, and each of the other professions.
The conception of the university as an ivory tower, as a
secular monastery or retreat is a repugnant one to me. The
university must indeed be in the thick of things. Otherwise it
tends to become irrelevant and the object of proper indifference.

There is no need to repeat here what I said about the
humanitarian function in an earlier chapter. It will suffice to
emphasize again that at its best the university's humanitarianism has been, first, finite in its scope and, second, indirect,
with carefully constructed intermediating agencies—such as
Extension divisions—serving as channels to the areas of
demand or desire. For the university to be involved in a few
substantial areas in this wise surely puts no strain upon the
nature of the university, and the areas themselves can often
prove of important worth to the university proper in its research and its teaching.

It is, however, a very different, potentially very damaging,
conception of the matter when the university feels obliged, or

allows itself to be driven to a constantly increasing number of these missions in society and, even more important, when it loses the profound and saving sense of intermediation, when an entire department, for example, declares itself concerned foremost with one or other of society's concrete problems— whether smog control or ethnic disadvantage. When this happens the department is lost and just another bureau is gained. That valuable knowledge regarding smog control can, in all hope, emerge from a chemistry department concerned with its usual spread of analytical problems is obvious. The same is true with regard to ethnic problems and the social sciences in the university. To build or adapt a single department around any such problem is, however, suicidal in the long run. The capacity of the American people for being concerned with "pressing social problems" is today beyond anything ever known in history. As Edward Banfield has emphasized in his *The Unheavenly City,* a great deal of both professional politics and of middle-class society generally is engaged in, incessantly engaged in, the meeting of problems. And if a given problem becomes dull to American consciousness (as the very crippling problem of alcoholism has become dull), then fresh and more arresting problems—such as marijuana, smog control, Negro uplift, and alienation of youth—must be quickly found.

The trouble with humanitarianism, once it seizes the mind, as it has the American mind, the *affluent mind,* is that there can be no such thing as a little. For no interest group relishes seeing some other group get attention when it does not. Once it enters the game, the university is put at the mercy of the politician and the interest group with political pressure. Day before yesterday this group was agricultural; yesterday, business and labor; today, ethnic; tomorrow, the breathers, the tasters, and hearers of atmospheric pollution.

And each one tends to leave its ineradicable bureaucratic framework, rarely if ever adaptable to distinctively different new pressures and needs. So does it, of course, in government. Who will forget rural electrification? But in government only the taxpayers' money is involved. And at the very least jobs are created. In the university this piling up of bureaucratic frameworks can make other activities—even those of research enterpreneurship and of political radicalism—difficult. I do not even mention teaching or scholarship.

Finally, there is no evidence that the academic individual comports himself with any greater ease and effectiveness in, say, the ghetto in pursuit of humanitarian university function than he does in government offices and committee chambers or among the revolutionary masses. The Agricultural Extension Service, at least for many years, had the wise requirement that its county agents had to have grown up on farms. This biographical attribute could not but have helped facilitate communication with the farmers. The Ph.D. in sociology or economics usually has little in either background or acquired manner that is likely to be of help along this line. He inspires resentment. He is bound to. And so, all too clearly, does the university itself, if only for the usually unfulfilled, perhaps unfulfillable, expectations its long-revered majesty in American society arouses.

Something should be said here about the single greatest— that is, in terms of political sensitivity—humanitarian problem the university has reluctantly taken on itself. I refer to direct action with the disadvantaged minority groups: Negroes, Puerto Ricans, Mexican-Americans, and possibly others. A great deal of pressure, from inside and from outside the university, is being placed on universities to admit, in constantly rising numbers, college-age youth from these groups who, solely by virtue of the appallingly inadequate educational rearing they have had, are manifestly not up to the standards of either admission or, once in the university, the grading of work.

Repeatedly we discover that a very large number of the college-aged members of these groups fail to reach the critical scores in the same entrance examination that have been taken immemorially by others. Granted that the admissions examinations themselves are far from perfect measures of general intelligence or capacity for achievement. Everyone knows that. Academic intelligence is a highly specialized type of intelligence. And it is not necessarily the best type. Criteria of success in these examinations tend to be, at least in some degree, drawn from white middle-class norms. All of this is to be granted readily.

Nevertheless, even after they are admitted, many in these ethnic groups are unable to hold their heads above water. By the traditional consensus of the academic community and the sanctions of the academic dogma, they are not admissible, nor, when admitted by humanitarian dispensation, able to perform at even minimally acceptable standard. Plainly, not all members of ethnic minorities fall in this category. Some have managed to achieve the necessary academic qualifications through clement home life, in which learning is respected and encouraged, or through unusually good, exceptional, schools. But as everyone acquainted with the problem knows, a substantial number do indeed fall in the category.

How do we meet the problem? Manifestly, it has got to be

met somewhere in society and soon. It has got to be met first and foremost in the ghetto schools, in the financially starved rural, and suburban, and urban sectors where for reasons all of us know the standards and the quality of education tend to be pitiful. This, however, is not my subject. My subject is solely the academic community. If the university is to be the means—the *humanitarian means*—of meeting the problem in any degree whatsoever, how, one is compelled to ask, can the university adapt itself to the needs involved and, at the same time, remain the institution to which members of the ethnic minority are attracted in the first place? All too clearly, it is one thing to be admitted to a fine municipal, state, or private university when one is admitted in terms of the same criteria applicable to all others. It is something else—for the institution *and for the person concerned*—when one is admitted by special standards which cannot fail to segregate, often cruelly, more cruelly to youthful minds than is the case in older, anticipated forms of segregation. It is one thing to receive a passing grade in a course when one knows he is being graded exactly as are the others in the class—that is, by the same standards. Clearly, it is something different, possibly humiliatingly different, when one becomes aware that his grade, indeed his academic survival, is an act of charity. A better recipe for the creation of long-run resentment and hostility to society would be hard to compose.

We are told that Montesquieu, when informed of the hostility in which he was held by another individual, asked: "Why? I have never done anything for him."

In whatever humanitarian capacity it works—agricultural, business, labor, or ethnic—it is hard for the university to avoid accumulating resentments almost in proportion to size of humanitarian endeavor. There are two reasons for this, one major, the other minor. The major reason is that the university's structure, its seemingly privileged ranks and roles, its continuing—if sharply diminished—sense of its own honor and of its qualitative superiority to other parts of society can no more avoid incurring resentments in the parts of the social order to which the university takes its humanitarian missions, than the university's resources, actual, finite resources, including its research and teaching, can avoid intolerable exploitation. The minor reason for the inevitable resentment the university will incur if it seeks to push any farther its humanitarian ventures is no more than the well-observed fact that such ventures, irrespective of the agencies representing them, accumulate hostilities toward the granting agencies in direct proportion to rising expectations. The university is ill-fitted to absorb these hostilities.

Finally, there is the close tie between modern humanitarianism and mass politics. It is almost always some ascendant political interest that is behind the university's venture into a new humanitarian sphere. In very large degree the politics of agriculture first led to the rise of agricultural experiment stations, agricultural extension services. And a succession of ascendant political interests has been largely responsible for the sequence of these humanitarian ventures ever since—right down to the present ascendancy of certain ethnic minorities. The point is, the university cannot hope to be its own master in this politically charged area. Each new humanitarianism will leave its almost predictably permanent structure behind, to remain long after either the need for or interest in the specific act of humanitarianism has vanished from the popular—and also academic—mind.

6

The university as therapeutic community. I will be extremely brief here, for I have already indicated in sufficient detail, it seems to me, the basic deficiencies of the university considered for very long as a setting for the cult of individuality. What seems almost invariably to happen in the programs, schools, and colleges founded to deal with real or imagined student needs of psychological character, such as identity crisis, is that the best lack all conviction and the worst are full of passionate intensity—to borrow the profound words of Yeats to good cause.

Within a short time the able faculty members, the bright and intellectually motivated students, who find themselves willy-nilly participating in these forms of communitarianism lose interest and, when opportunity permits, move to where challenging problems and situations can be found. The most dedicated in these programs are characteristically the least bright, the least intellectually oriented, and at their worst unable to concentrate mentally even to the point of reading a book. They require incessant attention, love, diversion, and companionship. Never having experienced authority in their homes, in many cases, they are incapable of enduring even the authority of an intellectual discipline in college. Easily, in fact almost chronically, bored, ever in search for some fresh diversion, some new form of "grooviness," finding temporary respite in the "soft" drugs such as marijuana (almost never the "hard" ones), such students are in search of a therapeutic community, not a university education. And, all too often today, they are encouraged in this search by their parents.

Two observations will suffice here. First, were it not for the immense intellectual prestige of the university, a prestige acquired, however, through intellectual-academic ways over the centuries, it is hardly likely that this breed of therapy-seeking middle-class students would come to the university at all. It is the combination of luster given the word "university" by great academic works, as well as by commanding position in American society during recent decades, and the breakdown of intellectual authority within the past decade or two, that alone makes possible the setting I speak of. If the university were to be conceived as entirely, as lastingly, dedicated to the cult of individuality, to ego needs, identity crises, and the like, it is hardly likely that it would retain the kind of prestige that today draws these students to it. The point is, no one wants to go to an asylum. But a great many will become interested in going to an asylum if it is called a university, has the accumulated luster of the university, and the historic freedom of movement within that goes with life in the university. Once however, it ceases to be possible to call the asylum a university, to bask, so to speak, in the glow of great learning, all the while not having to learn, the spell will be over. Community for its own sake has never proved to be of lasting interest in the history of human behavior. People come together, not to *be* together, but to *do* things that cannot be done alone.

The second observation can be succinct. It is simply inconceivable that the American people will very much longer remain in the roles of taxpayers or tuition-payers for the university conceived in this form. Their patience is vast but not limitless. As each fresh article in newspaper or newsmagazine describes some new college or program in a great university that has just abolished requirements, curriculum, examinations, grades, rules of any kind, and that declares itself dedicated to the ever loving, ever love-*needing* student (invariably white middle class), with his claimed identity crises "resulting from insufficient recognition at home and school," one keeps expectng the long-expected taxpayers, tuition-payers' revolt to manifest itself. It hasn't yet. But I think it can be assumed that it will.

❧ 13 ❧

THE FUTURE OF THE
ACADEMIC COMMUNITY

No ONE SERIOUSLY surveying the academic scene today can conclude other than that the American university is in an exceedingly precarious position. The luster of even the most historic and distinguished universities is fading rapidly. For the first time in the history of this country there is valid reason for wondering whether the university will survive. Alarmism may be the refuge of the timid, but any optimism at this time would be little more than euphoria. The blunt and inescapable fact is, the university in America is in the most critical condition of its history.

There are, as we have seen, many reasons for this. Most of them arise directly from the university itself: more especially from the profoundly dislocative changes during the past quarter-century that have led to fragmentation of its authority in society and to near-dissolution of its internal dogma and community. But there arc other reasons as well, proceeding from substantial changes in the nature of American business, professions, government, and culture at large resulting in ever more direct assumption by these areas of certain instructional and research functions heretofore lodged in the university alone.

All too plainly the university has become the object of contempt for many, including students, and of apprehension for others, including widening sectors of the pubic, nearly all of whom once regarded the university in America in much the way the Church was regarded during the Middle Ages.

The most serious mistake that any partisan of the university, or any one of its privileged citizens, could make would be to assume that "our affluent, technological, postindustrial society cannot possibly do without the university." This is both absurd and fatuously complacent. Of course, contemporary society could do without the university. What it cannot do without is knowledge: its ever continuing discovery and its constant diffusion to new generations. But to assume that only the university is qualified to perform this mission is as preposterous as it would have been for any sixteenth-century guildsman to assume that only through the craft guild could production of goods be continued. Other ways were then found. And other ways will be found—are already being found—to meet the research and teaching requirements of knowledge in our technological society.

The esteem in which a diploma from the American university has been held for generations is clearly diminishing. All the prestige of a Columbia, Harvard, or Berkeley degree could be wiped out in a decade, reduced to that of one or other of the spurious "schools" and "colleges" with which this country has been only too familiar in the past. Such effacements of prestige do not take long, once the processes begin.

The essence of our problem lies in the degradation of the academic dogma. Were it not for this degradation there would be little cause for apprehension at the present time. The university has been under assaults from the outside at other times in its history in America. Generally these had their origins in politically conservative sectors of society, in American business, and in the more fundamentalist parts of American religion. The university was under severe assault during the Depression 1930s, again for the most part from the right and with the added spur of widespread economic misery. But the power of these attacks notwithstanding, the university then had a solid and tough core of resistance: one formed by faculty members, administrators, students, and others who knew what the purpose of a university was, what it could rightly do and what it would risk its very soul by falsely doing.

It is with no desire to idealize that university and that academic community when I say that there was general, if usually unstated, awareness by scholars of the privileged position of the university in American society. There was awareness that the price of being able to engage in dispassionate scholarship and in rigorous, honest teaching was a fairly high one: this price was keeping the university as far as possible out of politics, out of economic enterprise, and, generally, out of the areas of society where partisan feelings are endemic, where passionate moralism is of the essence.

One may liken the situation to a kind of social contract. The academic community said in effect: if society will allow us the freedom to indulge ourselves in the aristocratic pleasures of seeking knowledge for its own sake and then teaching this to our students, we will stay as far as possible out of the areas of society in which, not dispassionate reason and

scholarly objectivity, but passionate moralism and politicization are incessantly required. And, allowing for the occasional
lapses, the social order generally agreed. The social contract
existed.

This did not mean, as I emphasized in the early chapters of
the book, the status of political eunuchs for American professors. Their isolation from politics has been grossly exaggerated by a present generation of faculty that mistakes
citizenship for unremitting political activism and that has
shown itself willing to carry on this activism in the classroom,
the learned society meeting, and even in the pages of sup-
posedly scholarly journals. From early times a sizable proportion of university faculty members and students engaged
in politics and in humanitarian work. But almost always with
a sense of limits, of proportion, of restraint. For these men
knew that despite any disclaimers they might make about
being "individuals not university members" when they engaged in business enterprise, substantial politics, or more or
less constant avocation of any kind, the university in a very
real sense went with them. There were exceptions, as there
always are. But not many.

The vital point, however, is not the degree to which individual faculty members indulged constitutional rights of citizenship off the campus. It is that it would never have occurred to even the most radical (or conservative) of these
individuals to seek to convert the university into a kind of
political engine. Or, for that matter, an economic engine.
Or a humanitarian or therapeutic engine. By all alike, radical,
liberal, and conservative, the purpose of the academic community was held to be simply and solely knowledge: its
discovery and its dissemination to students and to society

through teaching and publication. They did not need to be told how fragile this purpose was.

What is so widely called the crisis of the university today consists in this: we have lost the overarching sense of what the academic community is built upon; lost it in the flood of activities that began to permeate the academic community after World War II; activities I have described in detail under the headings of the higher capitalism, the new men of power, the cult of individuality, superhumanitarianism, and, above all, politicization.

What we are most concerned about as I write is, of course, the assaults upon the university of the New Left and, increasingly now, those of the political right. These dramatize and heighten the plight of the university. But they are not the essential causes of this plight. I do not underestimate either the New Left or the Far Right in American society. One would be a fool to do so. But I know that neither of these by now indubitably potent forces would have a fraction of its effect upon the university today were it not for the severely weakened position of the academic community that is the direct result of the forces I have described in earlier chapters. Our major weakness in the university at the moment is the nearly total lack of a sense of what the business of the university is, what its mission should be, what its distinctive contribution is to society.

If an institution, or anything, is what it does, how could one possibly work from the present jungle-like growths of use and function within the American university to any reasonably succinct definition. I realize that any major institution stands for a number of things, not just one. But always, except in times of crisis and extremity, there is some single, recognized, and inspiriting function that gives it its character, that supplies cement for human allegiances. Thus, no matter what range of things the family does for its members, we are in no doubt of what its central, its unique function is. And it is the continuing vitality of this function that will alone serve to keep in view, to hold in degree of importance, the other things the family represents. So too with the labor union. It is today engaged in social service, education, recreation, human relations, fund management, vacation resorts, and so on. But when its central purpose—that of protection of workers in industry—becomes dislodged, becomes extinguished by a competing institution, such as political government, or becomes overladen by its manifold secondary activities to the point where its central, sustaining function is no longer of importance to people, who can doubt that the labor union will go the way of the guild a few hundred years ago.

Exactly the same holds with the university. People will accept, or put up with, the variety of things done today in the university just so long as it has some distinctive, some motivating meaning or function that will seem to its members and also to society in general uniquely important. Mere number of activities will not save it from continuing degradation and eventual extinction. Of what advantage that it may manufacture research, produce athletic carnivals, service the needs of beet growers, lift up ethnic minorities, hold scientific conferences, do jobs for Defense or HEW, provide adolescent-sitting and role-therapy facilities at rates to parents, divert the public through either the public events provided by the Committee on Drama, Arts, and Lectures or those of more recent notoriety known as demonstrations and riots?

I grant that, recent turbulence notwithstanding, the luster

of the university in America remains impressive. If it didn't, there would be little use in even speculating about the future of the academic community. The glow under which a Harvard, Princeton, or Columbia, a Berkeley, Michigan, or Wisconsin, has lived for so many decades, even centuries, is not easily and quickly darkened. Assessed in terms of the number of scholarly light and leading at these places, along with the continuing appeal of the university in the minds of parents, the prestige of the university even today, after a decade of strife and storm, remains impressive.

But there is an old saying to the effect that the brilliance of foliage is never so great as just after the roots have been cut. There is much reason for believing the roots of the American university to be in very critical condition even if they have not yet been destroyed. Present convulsive conflicts—whether of authority, of function, or of meaning—in the university cannot go on indefinitely without lethal consequences. Some conflict, to be sure, is vital to any institution. It is the friction that produces energy as well as heat. And I am well aware how often merely latent or abstractly conceivable conflicts have a way of being resolved through what Burke called expediency.

But it is surely evident that conflict can be so great as to burst the walls of its containing structure. Conflict that is too deeply rooted, too long continued, too passionately expressed, becomes in due time what Aristotle called *stasis*. Of all dangers that society, especially democratic society, must face, wrote Aristotle, *stasis* is the greatest. For with this disease come all the familiar manifestations of consensus fragmented, purpose dislocated, and community dissolved. It is from *stasis,* Aristotle wrote, that there emerge those recurrent epochs of social and moral anarchy surmounted by absolute and repressive power.

The events of the past decade—and I am thinking here more of faculty response than I am of student insurrections—have made it clear that the university is as liable to the ravages of *stasis* as was the *polis* in ancient Greece.

2

Is the university today undergoing some possibly irreversible decline, comparable perhaps to what happened to the medieval Church, the guild, the landed aristocracy, and village community in earlier ages? Granted that pessimism is often belied by actuality. It is still true that major structures *do* occasionally break down or suffer fatal erosion. It is not difficult to imagine the seeming imperishability of the Church's power in the thirteenth and fourteenth centuries from the vantage point of some devout cleric or learned theologian. Or that of the merchant and craft guilds that were by then lying so profusely over the European landscape. Could any knight of that age, however perfect and gentle, have possibly foreseen the fate that would be his in the pages of Cervantes a couple of centuries later?

Great as the inherited luster is today of any one of our great universities, it would be absurd to suppose that there is any ineradicable position of strength, any endowed permanence, that it holds. Structures as great in nature and more powerful in expression than the American university have come and gone in history. Already the image of a Harvard that could rally the most powerful of its alumni before the threatened entry by a Senator Joseph McCarthy appears to be tarnished. The same is true of Yale, of Berkeley, of Wisconsin, of quite literally every major university in America at the present time. One has the sense of a constantly widening indifference, at best, to the university in the minds of Americans. I believe no people has ever lived that has had more pride in the idea of college and university, however naively expressed at times, than the American people. For how many families has the university or college been the very essence of Americans' dreams for their children? What pride was once taken in both admission and in graduation. The commencement ceremony had begun to assume almost ecclesiastical overtones, much like those of religious festivals in medieval Europe. Communities competed with each other for the privilege of being host to some new university or college or branch of established university.

Would anyone suggest that any, or much, of this is the case today? Probably not. And yet I think it would be a serious mistake to underestimate at least the *possibility* of the university's capacity to survive. Not all of the academic community is dissolved. Not all of the American public have become disgusted with the university. Most, I would judge, are more confused and bewildered than disgusted. The plant is there. The faculties and students are there. Applications for admission remain high. The diploma has not yet become a degraded piece of paper. American industry and government and the professions have not yet gone all the way in development of new sources, stable sources, of knowledge and of reliable means of training the young.

If a determining number of persons, chiefly the faculty in the university, will take the mighty step of seeking to arrest present processes of degradation and to form a fresh community of academic purpose, of newly affirmed academic dogma, there is no reason to suppose that disaster is—as it now would appear to be—inevitable.

3

What should the university be in the future? Stating the matter differently, what vitalizing function can be seen for the university that is alone capable, given the special character of its resources and character, of restoring academic authority and rebuilding academic community?

Keystone of the research establishment? But there are other organizations better qualified for this, given the technical requirements of large-scale research today. Adjunct government? But government has its own special demands and requires its own distinctive roles. And these appear ill suited to academic aptitudes. Radical critic or conscience of society? But societies do not generally support, with tenure, their radical critics; and anyhow there are more fertile contexts for the Gracchi, Robespierres, Benthams, Marxes, and Lenins of history. Supreme humanitarian, responsible for all of society's political, economic, and psychological ills and deprivations? The university is basically no more qualified for this than is either the church or the labor union. Therapeutic community designed to heal identity crises in middle-class youth? But even to the extent that this function may now be said to exist more or less successfully, it does so only in the reflected glow of the university believed to be a genuine intellectual community. Microcosm of culture, of the creative arts? To some extent, without doubt, but any thought of the university's cloistered community being seedbed for the Shakespeares, Mozarts, and Picassos of history, of providing necessary incentives, flies in the face of all that we know about the nourishing contexts of the arts in society.

I do not say that the university must rigorously eschew each or even all of these; that is, totally. I repeat: no great institution is ever cabin'd, cribb'd, and confin'd to but a single, narrowly conceived purpose or function. But no institution can remain either great or long in existence unless, giving structure to all its secondary or ancillary functions, there is some one, distinctive, and clearly perceived function; some purpose or meaning that casts its light over the social order. It is this function or purpose that I am concerned with in this final chapter. Whatever it is, if it is to have any semblance of realism and possibility of fulfillment, it must be one that has substantial relation to the trained capacities of those who work, live, and die in the university. Trained *in*capacities are an all too frequent occurrence in the history of culture; nowhere more evident than within institutions facing breakdown or *stasis*.

I suggest that the university's most feasible function for the future is in essence what it has been in the past: that of serving as a setting for the scholarly and scientific imagination. No doubt such a conception will seem archaic, off the main line of history, even reactionary to many of those who hold one or other of the conceptions I dealt with in the preceding chapter. But quite apart from the demonstrable (as I believe) infeasibility of these, why should the conception of the university as a setting for ideas, as a setting for both the discovery and the teaching of knowledge in the learned disciplines and professions seem anymore archaic today than it did three or four decades ago—at, say, Chicago, Berkeley,

Harvard, Columbia, or Caltech during any one of the great periods each of these, and many other universities have known?

What, in a civilized society, could possibly be wrong with, or stagnant, archaic, or antiquarian about, the vision of an enclave in the social order whose principal purpose is working creatively and critically with ideas through scholarship and teaching? Is not man's highest evolutionary trait thus far precisely his capacity for dealing with ideas: learnedly, imaginatively, and critically? Is there any more promising hallmark for a civilized society than its willingness to support a class of persons whose principal business is to think, to arrive at knowledge, and to induct others in this principal business?

Making exception only for the occasional periods of torpor, of desuetude in the university's long history, periods when its just reward was witnessing the light and leading of society doing their work outside the university's walls, this is precisely what the university has been about. The university is no monastery or retreat. And its business is the business of human life: *intellectual* business. But only as filtered and interpreted by the minds of those best qualified to distinguish the major from the minor, the important from the trivial, the relatively lasting from the manifestly transitory. It does not seem to me to matter very much what the intellectual content of a curriculum or course be so long as it is a subject clearly evocative to good minds and one on which a sufficient body of knowledge or informed understanding exists to provide the basis of intellectual discourse, of intellectual community. Much harm has been done to the university in times past by those who have tried to make the classics, say, or "liberal arts," or "general education," or perhaps some imagined need of the human personality the exclusive or chief subject of the university.

When Macaulay, no lover himself of the classical curriculum, was asked once why he nevertheless drew his recruits for the civil service from the classics at Oxford and Cambridge, he replied: "Because that is where the best students are. If instead of the classics astrology were the preferred subject I shouldn't mind. I would then seek out those students most proficient at casting nativities." Many crimes have been committed in the name of the classics and the liberal arts. At least some of the widening indifference of students to the university, especially in the nonprofessional areas, stems directly from subjects too long ritualized, their natural juices gone, their existence dependent almost wholly on curricular requirement.

This, however, is not the place to decide what subjects shall be the essential ones in the university. How, in any event, *could* one so decide: that is, abstractly? Subjects, courses, and curricula have changed frequently and diversely during the university's eight centuries of history. They have been and always should be resultants of what is going on in the whole area of creative scholarship, in the far larger area of creative imagination, and indeed in the largest area of all, that of human culture.

Our concern is none of these. It is the *mission* of the university, the *role* of the academic community in contemporary society. It is this, not intellectual content of the university, that is the source of the conflict presently threatening to destroy the structure of the university in America. Why must the proposal of an intellectual community, of a scene of ideas given structure by teaching and scholarship, be apologized for? Is it the radical function that is desired? But nothing is more radical than an idea. Is it the humanitarian function? Nothing in the long run is more humanitarian than a humane and moral idea. Is it citizenship? But no one can be a citizen simply by sedulously learning to be a citizen. The university's relation to government, research, the arts, and other great functions should be close. It always has been close in the university's brighter moments in history.

But close in ways that are germane to the character of the university. I have many times suggested there is something inherently aristocratic and guild-like about the university. And this has been as true of the great universities in times of creative ferment, right down to the Chicagos, Berkeleys, Harvards, and Michigans of the present century as it has of lesser universities in dull times. No genuinely intellectual community can possibly exist save in terms of an aristocracy that consists, basically, of no more than respect for the best ideas, scholars, and teachers, and the proper ranking of these with respect to those ideas, teachers, and scholars of lesser worth—as this worth is demonstrated within the academic community. Neither can any genuinely intellectual community survive without a system of authority, a system made legitimate by its clearly perceived relation to the function or purpose around which community and aristocracy alike are built.

Admittedly there is a degree of aristocracy that becomes mere privilege-claiming arrogance. And I noted in an early chapter of this book the degree to which the academic community in America has, in recent times, manifested such arrogance. So too is there a degree of guild-like authority, of emphasis upon structure and dominant purpose, that can only too quickly lead to a kind of complacent torpor of mind. All of this is true. But are we nevertheless to apologize for the idea of an intellectual aristocracy, one mindful of obligations as well as rights and privileges? I profoundly hope not. The highest goal of human culture is not obliteration of aristocracy: it is, so far as we can manage it, the basing of aristocracy on the levels of genuine intellectual and moral quality. Nor is there anything intrinsically wrong with the idea of either guild or community when we are thinking of contexts for the arts, letters, and sciences. Despite a romantic myth to the contrary a great deal of the world's most creative work, even in the spheres of music, painting, and literature, has been done in guilds and communities, however loose in structure some of these may have been.

4

Let us assume that the ideal of a community of ideas, undergirded by the primary functions of teaching and scholarship, is a worthy one for the university; not merely worthy but, if my argument has been reasonably correct, probably the only worthy one, all things considered. What, then, must be done to reestablish this academic community, to make it once again as evocative and creative as we know it to have been at other times in its long history. I suggest the following as being the prime requirements at the present time. They are requirements that confront the public, legislatures and government officials, boards of trustees, and students. But above any other single group in society it is the faculties of the universities that hold commanding position in the acceptance of, and then the implementation of these requirements. And among university faculties the crucial ones, clearly, are those in our most distinguished, our oldest and most prestige-laden universities. One must not ever underestimate the kind of influence that radiates from a Berkeley, Harvard, Columbia, Michigan, or Yale. As they go, so goes the academic nation.

What are the most fundamental requirements of the academic community and its rehabilitation in American life? I shall list them in the approximate order of their importance, or at least priority, seeking, of course, to make clear their relevance to the analytical discussion of earlier parts of this book.

1. *Repudiation of historicism.* This is vital, for already the air is full of proposals for the university each of which is said to be rooted in the "clearly developing character of the contemporary university." No mistake, however, can be greater than basing either proposal or analysis upon some imagined trajectory of development, upon what Sir Karl Popper has called historicism. Particularly pertinent here is prophylaxis against historicism regarding the university's role in politics, large-scale research, and humanitarianism. Each of these, as we have seen, has behind it large numbers of advocates. For them it is not enough that a certain proposal be desired or advocated. It must additionally be declared "inevitable" or "inexorable," the consequence of its being pulled by the locomotive of history down a single track bed. Failure to hook on to the locomotive of history results, it is said, in being condemned to archaism, in being reactionary or nostalgic. How many follies and knaveries in history have been committed by those in supposed possession

of the "track of history" it would be impossible to guess. But the number is large.

And of all dangers confronting the university today in American society the greatest is, I believe, the habit of assuming that some indwelling pattern of development exists and that planning for the university must be in accord with this pattern. Given this habit of mind, certain consequences follow. One sees the individual making the pronouncement walking through university halls, in effect, saying: "This is traditional and must go; this is modern and must be lived with no matter how ugly; this is early future and must be built upon." The things found in a university are thus declared, not simply good and bad, but inevitable or modern, on the one hand, and, on the other, traditional or archaic. How preposterous!

One must indeed begin with existing realities. And, clearly, it is as fatuous to plan around something traditional because it is traditional as around some figment of the imagination deemed to be the inevitable future. I am referring only to the present, widespread habit of condemning to the lumber room of history academic ends that plainly continue to be worthy ones, plainly command allegiance and respect from both faculty and students, but that, by their age, receive the epithet "traditional" and, hence, the all-out curse "obsolete." The first and indispensable step, then, in reform of the university is abandonment of historicism. The sole objective of planning should be simply the highest possible combination of the desirable and the feasible.

2. *The restoration of authority.* Nothing else can be achieved until the university is able to create again a system of recognized authority such as it had down until a decade

or two ago. Despite commencement speeches of university presidents during the past two decades to the contrary, the distinctiveness of the university has never lain in what it taught and studied. It lay in its unique structure of authority for generation after generation: a structure of authority that was itself built on the cherished authority of reason and knowledge. There was never anything perfect or puncture-proof in this authority. Nor should there have been. We are talking about universities, ever the scene of periodic eruptions of one kind or other, not asylums, monasteries, or prisons. But the kind of chaos, flouting of authority as supreme objective, buckling of legitimate centers of authority in the university, in short, collapse of authority save as it is undergirded by police, we have seen for nearly ten years now is clearly insupportable from any point of view.

The first stage of this rehabilitation of legitimate authority lies in endowing the formal administration of the campus with the priority and freedom from incessant veto powers by faculty and students that formal administration in the American university once had. Not least among the degradations of the academic scene in America during the past quarter-century has been the degradation of, first, department chairmen, then deans, then presidents. For a long time this degradation of role and authority was rationalized in terms of faculty participation in the university's system of authority. And, as I stressed in Chapter 3, a good university is simply inconceivable apart from a substantial measure of reliance upon faculty judgment in those areas—curriculum, academic policy, above all, appointments and promotions of faculty, and admissions of and degrees and certificates granted to students—where it is uniquely informed and therefore vital.

But by the same token no great university has ever been achieved in this country without the leadership that flowed from relatively strong administrators, particularly presidents. It is not merely that Harvard, Berkeley, Chicago, Cornell, and other universities became distinguished under the leadership of strong presidents such as Eliot, Wheeler, Harper, and White; it is that they only succeeded in remaining great for long periods as the result in very large degree of this leadership. And, as the veriest novice in the study of administration knows, no administration can become effective over a long period of time if its every act is under the *de facto,* if not *de jure,* veto power of faculty committees whose powers are inevitably surer in matters of consultation, leisured advice, than in matters of direct administration.

This is the first necessity: the restoration of the authority of the president of the university, and of the provosts, deans, and department chairmen, in whose hands responsibility is placed for the governance of the university. This carries with it, of course, the corollary that boards of trustees and—as in public institutions—political figures in legislative and executive offices of government will be obliged to give firm backing to university officials. As matters now stand, the university president is as often rendered impotent by failure of key public, or trustee, figures to back him in time of crisis as by failure of faculty.

There will be nothing easy in this restoration of authority to presidents and deans. On a score of grounds such restoration will be attacked from one end as invasion of faculty and student democracy and, from the other, as signal to fresh outbursts of revolt. But apart from such restoration I do not see how the university can do what it is supposed to do academically or how it can hope for the rather privileged enclave-like status that is the real structure of its freedom in society.

The faculty has the most to learn here. Few things have done more in recent years to undermine the authority of the university than the wanton spreading of the view that the faculty, *qua* faculty, must concern itself with each and every aspect of administrative life on the campus. It has led men and women whose sole claim to distinction is as teachers and scholars into areas of governance and responsibility for which they are largely unfitted by temperament and by principal interest. The revolt at the present time of students against administration had, as its immediate prelude, the more subtle but nonetheless puissant revolt of the faculty against the administration—a revolt characterized by spreading, deepening faculty insistence that all spheres of the university, student discipline, management of residence halls, and the scores of other spheres that exist, that are bound to exist on a university campus in our century, must be brought continuously under faculty scrutiny and direction.

No good university can conceivably exist unless the *de facto* authority of the faculty is very great in matters of appointment and promotion of colleagues, in admissions, in the granting of degrees, and in curricular matters. These, after all, are the sovereign elements of the academic community. But there is, on the evidence of the history of the university, a price that must be paid for the faculty's dominance in these crucial areas. And that price is forebearance from insistence upon dominance in each of the multitude of other, secondary, ancillary areas of the university.

No good university is, ever has been, or conceivably could

be a direct and total democracy. One cannot devote himself effectively to teaching and scholarship if he must be forever sniffing out possible derelictions of those whose job it is to supervise plant and facilities, the social and moral behavior of students, athletics, relationships with trustees and alumni. If the professor's authority in study or classroom is to remain great, he can hardly subject it to the inevitable follies and errors that must attend efforts to make this authority equally great in the nonacademic areas of the university.

That presidents, provosts, deans, and department chairmen err, sometimes grievously, is obvious enough. And when they err too frequently, over too long a period of time, they must be replaced. This is clear enough to be elementary. It has always been this way. Equally clear and elementary, however, is the fact that a perpetual, incessant, ever potentially decapitating mass democracy on the campus will serve only to discourage the gifted from departing their own classrooms and studies for the tasks of administration that are, even at best, onerous and unblessed by thanks. The overwhelming majority of those, even today, who enter the academic profession do so for reasons unrelated to desires to be either administrators or political activists—taking that last in the full, including intramural, sense of the term. How attractive can the university be to the genuinely academic temperament if life within it must be a constant succession of crises precipitated by efforts at direct and total democracy on the part of the faculty.

Today the faculty's authority, in even the areas most vital to its and the university's existence, is at an all time ebb. A great deal of this ebb is to be attributed to the debasing and the dissipating consequence flowing from extension of faculty authority into areas of the university so numerous, so diverse, often so trivial, really, that residual authority cannot help but be demeaned.

Much nonsense is being spoken these days about student rights to participate in the government of the university. One even finds spokesmen for the view that students should sit on governing boards, highest faculty councils, the committees concerned with appointment and promotion of faculty, the approval of courses, and so on. All this for a group that by its very nature is transitory in the university: four or five years at most for any given student and the ever present possibility of dismissal for demonstrated ignorance and incompetence. That students have a collective right to have their scholarly interests treated seriously; a right to make their views known to faculty and administration; a right to be spared the childhood-perpetuating restrictions and indignities that used to be heaped upon them in the name of *in loco parentis;* a right to speak out (even if not a divine right to be listened to incessantly); a right to participate as they see fit in political and other activities outside the university, subject as adults to the laws of civil society and recognizing that the university cannot be their sanctuary too: all of this I take to be so valid as to be scarcely worth the emphasis here. Above all, from the point of view of the practical reinforcement of the faculty's teaching responsibilities, students have the right—I would say duty—to evaluate and assess as best they can, as effectively, even loudly, as they can, the quality of the teaching they are getting. I shall say more about this below.

But it is utter nonsense to suppose that students, none of them likely to be present on the campus for more than four or five years at most, their responsibility for the campus accordingly diminished, should participate at high and crucial levels in the formal government of the university, either within administrative or within faculty councils. Any effort so to suppose can only result in persuading students that what they are clearly *not* qualified to assess—levels of knowledge in a field, scholarly stature of professors, relation of courses to the state of knowledge, among other spheres— is more important than what they are qualified to assess.

The vital point though is restoration of authority. Without such restoration of authority there is no possibility of arresting present encroachments upon the autonomy of the university: encroachments by legislature, governor, federal agency, and police. And these encroachments are becoming as plain in the private universities as in the public. The chief consequence of breakdown of authority within an institution is invariably the rise of power, whether from within or outside. If members of the university faculty are unwilling to make a major distinction between the (admittedly fallible) authority of president, dean, or department chairman, on the one hand and, on the other, the power of the police, they are sure to get ever greater amounts of the latter.

3. *A clearing of the scene.* I do not see how either academic authority, teaching, or any other vital aspect of the university can be long maintained without the removal of a substantial number of present structures and activities on the American campus within the next ten years. On a rough guess I should think at least 75 percent of all existing institutes, centers, and bureaus, in the academic sphere of the university should be phased out. There is no need to repeat here what was said in earlier chapters about the toll taken by the higher capitalism in the university, as well as

by the university's ill-advised effort to become adjunct government and superhumanitarian for American society. To these might be added the now multitudinous faculty consultantships and other forms of moonlighting through which high academic salaries are augmented. Such consultantships, despite self-justifying myth to the contrary, are rarely useful to scholarship and almost always prejudicial to teaching.

It is not research, large or small, that I want phased out of the university. God forbid. Research, along with teaching, is what universities are all about. But again I say, research-in-teaching and teaching-in-research, and of a scale that does not constantly threaten to dwarf the rest of the university! I am well aware that there is much research today that simply cannot be done except in vast, highly organized bureaucratized centers. Very good. But let such research be done where it can be done more efficiently and without damage to academic community. And let those whose passions are directed toward this kind of research be free to move from the university. Make no mistake. A substantial number will choose to move, including some of highest luster.

Make no mistake either about the powerful resistance that will be mobilized immediately against this clearing of the scene: by trustees, faculty, and graduate students, among others, not to emphasize those in the great foundations, major departments of government, and others whose vast funds have made the jungle of institutes possible. The cries of status-pain, of income-pain, of power-pain will be awful to have to listen to. It is inconceivable to me that the work of clearing the scene of the thick overgrowth of institutes and centers along with the many other forms of organized distraction from teaching and of organized depredation upon the academic community, could be done by any one university alone. My guess is that, given the very deep roots and very wide spread these organizations and activities have at the present time, only concerted action by the top twenty or thirty universities in the country would bear substantial result. If this be conspiracy. . . .

To a large, powerful, and highly vocal number of faculty members any such phasing out of the higher capitalism, adjunct government, and superhumanitarianism will seem intolerable tyranny. It will be called unscrambling of eggs, an effort to return to the Middle Ages, a turning of clocks backward, and—most powerfully—a failure to recognize the track on which the locomotive of history is running. In fact, as I think on the sheer amount of faculty income, wealth, and, perhaps above all, faculty sense of status, that is today based upon institute, center, and professional consultantship, along with the many other manifestations of the higher capitalism and superhumanitarianism I have written of, I do not think a clearing of the scene is at all likely.

But I do not see how any genuine academic community, any genuine restoration of academic authority, or any substantial elevation of the function of teaching and of critical concern with ideas can take place until the scene has been cleared.

4. *The depoliticization of the university.* The university is today suffused by politics; this includes the private as well as the public university. I use the word "politics" in every significant sense that word could have for the university. The number of laws and administrative regulations affecting university operation that stem from federal and state governments is at an all-time high. This is the consequence of, first,

the higher capitalism in the university, involving the multitude of financial relations with agencies of government, and, most recently, of the apprehension created in the public mind by the turbulence of the 1960s. There is no need to emphasize the degee to which the campus has become a microcosm of the national and international scene in the number and intensity of ideological issues it has assimilated during the past two decades. And, finally, no one can miss the extent to which "participatory democracy" in university affairs has not only, as I just noted, sapped the foundations of any coherent system of authority, but also created a setting of instant and chronic politics that increasingly makes serious teaching and study impossible.

I do not see how the university can conceivably fulfill the mission of detached teaching and scholarship, of objective study of ideas and values, within circumstances such as those prevailing at the present time. I suggested above that the earlier autonomy of the university in American society, its fairly substantial freedom to engage in the teaching and research that it chose to engage in, was the consequence of a kind of social contract. By virtue of reasonable forebearance from the passions of the political scene and of delegating to administration the operating responsibilities of the university, the faculty and students received from society a kind of mandate for carrying on university teaching and study; a mandate that left the university largely free of invasion from partisan sources outside. Naturally, this social contract was never a perfect one. Threats to academic freedom existed from time to time. Both faculty and students participated in political, religious, and other activities outside the university, though very moderately by present standards. Still something approximating this social contract existed, and within it the university flourished.

Is resumption of such a contract possible today? Putting the matter differently but crucially, is a depoliticization of the university possible? It is very hard to see much possibility of this. Once politicization becomes deeply ingrained, once federal and state governments are in the habit of penetrating any cultural or social sanctuary, once members of an organization begin to define their very constitutional status as citizens in terms of incessant political activism, and once the normal hierarchy of the academic community has been seriously weakened by spreading habits of participatory democracy, first among faculty, then among students, with all offices under a kind of standing suspicion, all decisions subject to threat of veto action, the likelihood of arresting these tendencies is not very great. There is much in history to give substance to that conclusion. But of the importance of depoliticization there can be no question.

5. *The elevation of the function of teaching.* I should stress the fact that I am referring here to the function of teaching; that is, the activity itself, as it is regarded by the academic community. I am not referring to the largely futile efforts to persuade individuals—through annual awards, occasional salary increases, homilies on the subject from administrators, and the like—that teaching is important when the entire weight of evidence in the contemporary university is that teaching is not important.

The function of teaching was degraded when, following World War II, the function of project-, or grant-, or institute-based research became the only genuinely valued function; when it became possible to win renown, high salary, and power in the university without more than a kind of token appearance in classroom and seminar. Of what avail is it today solemnly to remind young instructors of their "teaching obligations"; of what use is it for students to assess faculty performances; and of what incentive is it to offer annual teaching awards, when the evidence is so clear as to be blinding that through research alone one moves into the upper levels of success. I see no reason for repeating here any of what I dealt with in detail earlier in the book. It is enough to observe once again that today, so far as the large mass of students are concerned, the conspicuous abrogation of distinguished faculty members from the historic priority of teaching is without any question the chief source of the bitterness one finds among these students at one extreme and the spreading cyncism regarding the purpose of the university at the other.

How do we elevate the function of teaching to the point where the average is at least as high as it was down until World War II? Here again we are involved in special interests, accumulated privileges and luxuries, as well as status values, that make any thought of an easy answer absurd.

The first and, I believe, most fundamental approach lies in what I called above the clearing of the scene. There cannot be any honoring of teaching so long as there is left in existence the whole, vast structure of research-dominated—especially large-scale research-dominated—institutes and centers that tower above all else in the university today in America. Add to this structure the diverse range of consulting, entrepreneurial, and humanitarian activities carried on in industry, government, and the professions by individual faculty members. Until this thick overgrowth is cleared it is difficult to see how the function of teaching can again become an honored one on the American campus. Here, amid all these post-World War II opportunities for the acquisition of wealth and status, lies the present degraded status of teaching.

The second requirement for the elevation of the function of teaching is the elevation once again of the department— school, college, whatever it is called—in which teaching and research are joined indissolubly. For, as recent history has demonstrated, once they are separated, with teaching held the responsibility of one kind of unit and research another kind, invidious distinction is inevitable. The worst possible approach to the matter is the establishment of special schools or colleges in which, as it is solemnly said so often today, "teaching, not research, will be made the sole function." Good students want to be where the intellectual action is. They do not want to be shunted off into areas that are eschewed by the light and leading of the faculty and that within a short time begin to resemble, at one extreme, educationists' experiments and, at the other, an asylum for the retarded.

The third requirement for the elevation of the teaching function is restoration of the kind of academic contract with faculty members that once was universal: that is, one in which a full load of teaching is required irrespective of the research or professional status of the faculty member, a load that cannot be escaped through the presently easy outlets of joint appointments in institutes and centers. Nor through titles of "Research Professor." Nor through term or annual leaves of absence that, given the sufficiency of foundation funds these days for the elect in academia, so often make a mockery of allegedly continuing professorships. Nor through any of the other by now well-known, easily available (to the scholarly and scientific elect, that is) opportunities for reducing teaching presence in classrooms and seminar down to a scant minimum.

It may be—it will be—said that the effect of the above can only be to diminish seriously the amount of research done in the university. I deny it. There is not a shred of evidence to support the view that this generation of scholars and scientists in the university is more creative, more productive in the valid sense of the term, than was the generation that preceded World War II: a generation in which not all the research eminence imaginable freed a senior scholar from a load of teaching that was commonly three courses in the humanities and social sciences and two courses in the laboratory disciplines: courses, by the way, that were rather evenly distributed between undergraduate and graduate areas and that continued year after year.[1]

Bear in mind that none of the above requirements is guaranteed to convert a dull teacher into a bright one, or to assure appointment in the first place of the good and distinguished in the ranks of teachers. But what *is* guaranteed to accomplish this? There were, as I emphasized early in the book, dull and mediocre teachers in the traditional university. Who did not know them? But it is a fairly safe generalization that the proportion of reasonably good teachers is

[1] The University of Chicago, which during its great years 1915–1930 was probably the single most creative academic center of thought and teaching this country has yet known, did not, if I am correctly informed, have even a sabbatical leave policy. "We come to teach" was the refrain one heard from even the most notable and creative of scholars and scientists.

bound to be a great deal higher when teaching a full load is made a *sine qua non* of academic status, when the present large number of easy escapes from teaching is reduced, and when the very structure of the university makes certain that teaching is honored in fact, not merely in homily and ritual award.

Equalization of the functions of scholarship and teaching is no doubt an impossible ideal. In fact, as one thinks about the matter, it is hardly to be considered an ideal. The man of distinguished ideas, of notable scholarship or science, should be, and almost certainly will be, more honored in the university community than the man of more ordinary intellectual contributions who is widely known for effective classroom performance. The highest places in the academic hierarchy of the traditional university were almost invariably reserved for the great scholar or scientist. This is as it should be. And in any event there is no way by which we can, Canute-like, decree the equality of teaching and research in the university.

Such degree, or even goal, is not the point. One can live well enough in an academic environment in which individual teaching takes its chances through the more or less normal processes of the free market. It is only when the whole immense structure of tariffs, quotas, monopolies in favor of research alone, ushered into the American university through the higher capitalism, makes any thought of a free market an absurd one, that teaching becomes degraded to the point where not all the individual awards, salary bonuses, and special asylums imaginable can be of any help.

6. *A finite conception of the university.* This may well be the most difficult of all the requirements to meet, for

what has somehow developed in the American mind, academic and nonacademic, is a nearly Faustian view of the university and its potential benefactions. It is difficult to see how academic policy can operate any more effectively than foreign policy without some constraining sense of limits. The kind of transcendent moralism that democracy has tended from the beginning to invest in our view of political government and of the role of political democracy in the world is to be found in full glory today in the university and in popular assessments of the university.

It is no more possible for the university to serve all individual needs and tastes than it is possible for it to serve all social, economic, and political needs in society. The sound democratic conviction that all persons should have reasonably equal access to the university has unfortunately become converted in recent decades to the dangerous—because of inherent impossibility of ever fulfilling it—conviction that the university must be incessantly reshaped to meet all possible interests and needs. So long as these are genuinely intellectual and academic interests and needs, no great problem is created. The progress of the university has consisted exactly in the changes and adaptations of curriculum necessary to meeting them.

It is clearly a different matter, however, when to the intellectual-academic function of the university there is added a set of other functions ranging from the spiritual and moral to the psychological and the social. A great deal of what I earlier referred to in the book as the cult of individuality is a direct response to the entrance in ever widening numbers of students who have little if any interest in the university as a setting for study in the learned disciplines but who must be—

or so the familiar argument runs—given incentive, be made interested, be provided with something deemed relevant, be, at all costs, entertained. It is the unhappy fate of the once honored liberal arts to have become the repository for most of these students, and I can think of nothing that has so hastened the degradation of this sector of the university than the heavy pastoral responsibilities that have been dumped on the liberal arts by the Faustian conception of the university. Today, as is all too evident, even the standard areas of the liberal arts prove insufficient. Hence the turning by desperate administrations and faculties to still more accessible, still more "relevant" types of course and curriculum. Hence the vogue of quasi-therapeutic sensitivity and encounter classes, of courses built around direct intuition or feeling in which all members of the academic community are indeed equal. And as these last become, as they show clear signs of already becoming, contexts of fresh boredom, and as fresh demands arise for novel diversion "relevance," it is anyone's guess what the university will next turn to for purposes of pacification.

I emphasize that I am *not* here suggesting that the problem of the university lies foremost in the admission of the mentally unqualified, the intellectually inferior. Far from it. I am inclined to think in fact that the problem lies more often in the admission, through false pretenses by the university, of those who are in a certain sense too bright, too gifted, too filled by intellectual passion already reached, for the inherently limited capacities of any curriculum to satisfy.[2]

[2] Basically, it is not "brightness" in its several degrees of academic assesment that is the crux of the matter. It is, rather, varying, diverse *types* of mind and motivation which can, for present purposes, be stipulated as of equal brightness.

To return once again to the distinction I made early in the book between the two traditions in the West, the first essentially that of charisma and direct creative or prophetic power, the second one of learning patiently accumulated, of scholarship, of study of data and text. It is not necessary to declare these rigorously separated from one another—which would be absurd—to see that substantial differences of mind are involved in the two traditions: differences of mind and of aptitude and of goal.

Even during its brightest and most creative moments the university, by its rather communal and corporate nature, has never been the home of all the light and leading in the West. Can one easily imagine a Buddha, Moses, or Jesus, an Aeschylus, Chaucer, or Shakespeare, a Bach, Mozart, or Beethoven being improved by enforced, or falsely motivated, residence in a curricular setting with all its requirements and blocks to individuality? Plainly not. I am not suggesting at all that genius is some purely internal or genetic thing, without need of contexts. I am suggesting only that the university is by no means the proper context for any and all forms of intellectual endowment.

In exactly the same way that the university is not, on the evidence, the best setting for the creative writer, musician, and artist, so perhaps is it not the best setting for the maturation of a few other, equally important if not as vivid, types of mind and personality in society. It was not from lack of mental endowment that a Marco Polo would have been ill-placed in one of the universities of his day—or, later, any one of the *philosophes,* or a Bentham, or a Marx. Each one of these might conceivably have improved the university he went to, but it is exceedingly unlikely that the university could have added a cubit to his stature.

Is the possibility not equally great in the fields of business and the practical arts generally that the university, far from being vital to personal success, is more often an organized, socially sanctioned means of deferment of personal success? Except in certain highly specialized areas which are comparable to law or engineering, is it really any more important that the businessman spend four years of tedium in the liberal arts than that the professional superstar in athletics spend four years in a college or university? Heaven knows, one of the reasons why the costs of universities have soared is the exploitative uses business and professional athletics— and many other areas of American life, including American families looking for havens for their adolescents—make of the university.

Once, no doubt, college or university was a unique way by which the merely literate could be given at least speaking acquaintance with the wide world of culture, that is, high culture. This is certainly no longer the case. There is a great diversity of ways by which the modern media and other institutions perform this function, and very often better than it can be done by the university.

One of the most encouraging movements that could take place in this country would be a major deemphasis in the business world on the university diploma, on "credentialism" generally. As Dael Wolfle has very recently pointed out, studies show that there is indeed a high correlation between college graduation and career income; but these studies, properly made, also show that what appears to be the central role of the college degree is in fact the central role of the brighter mind. There are assuredly occupational areas where university or college education is important. University teaching, law, medicine, engineering are all obvious in this regard.

There are far more areas, however, where the diploma is a mere employment screening device, without much relation, as Dr. Wolfle notes, to the substantive issues involved. "To deemphasize credentialism will require that employers make greater efforts to evaluate applicants as individuals instead of treating them as members of educational classes." [3]

I cannot help thinking that the great structure of occupations in this country and, not least, the lower socioeconomic and ethnic groups struggling to get into the higher reaches of this structure, would be immensely advantaged if a more finite view of the university were to be taken. I have already stressed the harm that has been done both university and many interest groups in our society by the university's assumption of the role of superhumanitarian. No less harm is being done both university and many a bright, motivated, aspiring young mind by the once useful but now all too often harmful adjuration: "Get a college education."

If the limits of the university are to be as wide as those of modern society and culture, then there is really no need for the university at all. Whatever the tasks of training necessary to fitting individuals to jobs, these can be, as can the requisite search for knowledge necessary to technological survival, carried on within the precincts of occupation, profession, or social and cultural interest.

Far more deadly to the character of the university than its exploitation in economic terms is its exploitation in psychological terms. That is, cultivation of the pernicious idea that by sending young people to universities one is teaching them to be human beings, to become citizens, to become leaders, or to find peace of mind, individuality, liberal arts,

[3] Dael Wolfle, "Overeducation" in *Science,* April 17, 1970.

"soul," or whatever may be in the public mind at the moment.

It is simply impossible for the university to be anything and, at the same time, to be all things; to meet any personal needs and, at the same time, to meet all imaginable personal-psychological-social-cultural needs. There is no reason, however, to repeat again what I have said sufficiently often in this book. It will suffice to say that one of the highest of all priorities for rehabilitation of the university as the setting for ideas, as the scene of teaching and scholarship in the learned disciplines, is abandonment of the present limitless, boundless, Faustian conception of the university and its relation to man and society.

5

Can these requirements for the rehabilitation of the university be feasibly met during the next few years—or, for that matter, any requirements designed to restore to the university the status it once had as enclave for teaching and scholarship in the humanities and the sciences? I hope so. I do not know. Who could know? At the moment, all considered, it seems highly unlikely. I will conclude where I began the book: by noting the increasing intensity of the conflict between the structure of the university, the purpose and mission of the university as these are readily translatable into the kinds of roles and statuses we find in the university, and the whole gathering fury of the winds of modernity. Very probably the New Left, for all its disdain of history save as weapon of political combat, has, down underneath its rhetoric, a surer sense of this mounting conflict than most of those who love, or profess to love, the university. The left can echo Voltaire's *"Ecrasez l'Infâme"* with reasonable certainty that the university in America today has, by virtue of the higher capitalism and the other structural characteristics it has taken on during the past quarter-century, as precarious a relation to modernity as the corrupt Church had in the eighteenth century.

The essence of the problem of the university lies in the fact that it has ceased to be the quasi-medieval, characteristically aristocratic entity that it was through its entire history, down until about World War II, but it has not become wholly modern: modern in the social, cultural, and intellectual senses of this word. And its problem is heightened by the fact that all efforts to become modern—in the sense, say, that the Air Force, General Motors, CBS, the Mayo Clinic, the Ford Foundation, HEW are modern—are crippled at the outset by the trained incapacities of this generation of university faculty and students for becoming modern.

I have said that the role of professor is today as deeply damaged—damaged by the currents of change described above—as the role of guildsman, knight, or landed aristocrat was damaged by the changes which were eventually to yield Western society its ages of capitalism, nationalism, democracy, socialism, and its several other sequences or phases of the history of modernity. Clearly, however, it does not follow that the contemporary professor will disappear overnight. The knight didn't; neither did the proud guild master. And, as we know, there are still remnants of the landed aristocracy to read about in the English press. Even guild halls have their uses, as every American tourist knows. No one can know how much longer the university can survive as an institution, how much longer the roles of professor, dean, chancellor, and the others that form university structure will continue to evoke at least a spark of public recognition. All efforts to read the future are either games or else tricks played upon the naive. I prophesy neither doom nor future glory for the university in America. I do not prophesy.

We do know certain things, however, We know that the guildsman did not become the capitalist entrepreneur; that the knight did not become the foot soldier or the artilleryman; that the landed aristocracy, while it may indeed have financed a great deal of the capitalist system, did not become the bourgeoisie; that, in sum, the roles and structures of medieval society did not themselves become the roles and structures of modern industrial and democratic mass society.

There is no inherent, self-sustaining, irresistible majesty in the university; only the majesty that is conferred upon the university by a social order that, for whatever reason, has come to believe that there is something distinctive, something precious, something profoundly important in the university that is to be found nowhere else in society—not in factory, not in foundation, not in government agency, not in media, not in church, not in mental health clinic, not anywhere else. And when this belief is allowed to erode, majesty erodes with it.

The greatness that is Harvard and the glory that is Berkeley can perish in but a few years, their presently celebrated degrees the objects of ridicule, their halls untenanted by any of the illustrious, their mission degraded to the caring, the feeding, and the policing of the young. Not even the young, though, will long choose to stay at Harvard and Berkeley once the word gets around that history has passed the universities by, that what the universities have to offer is no longer valued deeply either by those inside the university or those outside. History is filled with degrees, titles, ranks, and diplomas that were once thought to be important but that became in due time, after their functional importance had disappeared, mere curiosities or relics.

I do not prophesy this for the university in America. I do not prophesy at all. There is no way of knowing what profound changes of mind regarding the university will take place in faculties, boards of trustees, professional societies, and others traditionally responsible for the status of the university in American society. But I know this: the university in its present form is as nearly hopeless a structure as one can easily imagine. Its inner community and its traditional authority fragmented by the changes following World War II, its direct contribution to the social order a now visibly diminished one, its ancient dogma of knowledge for the sake of knowledge the object of derision, its curriculum and its sense of intellectual mission objects of contempt from both the political left and the right and—far, far worse—of spreading indifference inside and outside its walls (it is indifference, not anger or hate, that kills great institutions), the university in America today is plainly in as critical a position as was the guild or any knightly, aristocratic order in post-Reformation Europe.

If it be said that the sheer volume of capital represented by university plant and equipment should be sufficient to maintain the university permanently in American society, I can only point to the equal volume of capital—relatively speaking—once expended on pyramids, coliseums, and cathedrals in the West, now gathering places for tourists and other sight-seers. If it be said that surely *some* use will have to be found for the laboratories, classrooms, dormitories, faculty clubs, and student unions, I can only say that "some" use is not precisely what we are concerned with at the present time in discussions of the future of the American university. After all, there is no reason why all of these could not be used effectively, and at low-cost purchase, by business corporations, penological systems, the armed forces, and professional athletic teams. There is no easily seen end to the possibilities of use of plant and equipment in the contemporary university. They are not, however, what a university, or any form of cultural and intellectual community is about.

EPILOGUE

Twenty-five hundred years ago a dogma was born among the Greek rationalist philosophers. The dogma said: "knowledge is good." Not necessarily knowledge in service to self-survival, nor to power, nor to affluence, nor to religious piety; but knowledge in its own service. The kind of knowledge that springs from the itch of curiosity, from dispassionate, disinterested desire to obtain objective knowledge of nature, society, and man.

From the beginning this dogma has proved to be a fragile one. It has been almost constantly assaulted by those unable or unwilling to comprehend why knowledge should be its own end, why knowledge should ever serve ends other than of physical survival, political power or revolution, religious doctrine, economic affluence, and the whole broad spectrum of needs, desires, and passions of day-to-day living.

The dogma of knowledge did not even survive Greek civilization. The time came, a time aptly characterized by Sir Gilbert Murray as one of failure of nerve, when it was choked off, suffocated, by beliefs that found their essence in consecrated irrationalism, superstition, myth, and worship of power.

Not until the twelfth and thirteenth centuries in Western

Europe did the dogma of knowledge and its supporting ties of reason and objectivity find secure resting place. This was in the newly founded university. At first a local guild, confined to but a handful of towns such as Bologna, Paris, Oxford, and Salamanca, the university became within a century or two one of the most powerful communities to be found in the long history of Western man. Not only was the university powerful; it proved to be astonishingly fertile. Where at first there were only a few of its type, there soon were dozens, then hundreds, eventually thousands—in Western Europe, Eastern Europe, the Americas, Asia, the Middle East, Oceania, and Africa.

Some of the universities were distinguished centers of ideas and teaching from the very beginning. Others proved to be mediocre throughout their history; some, alas, were exceedingly poor in quality, monuments to dullness of mind. But what all the universities had in common, irrespective of quality, was dedication to the quest for knowledge, to the ideal of dispassionate reason: that is, to the dogma of knowledge that had first been brought into being by the pre-Socratic Greeks. Around this dogma had developed, by the thirteenth century, the academic community; one proud in bearing, unique in purpose, and, as we know, capable of exerting great influence, of arousing great respect and allegiance, wherever it was to be found. Soldiers, bishops, merchants, even kings and popes found it expedient to court the university at times and to treat it with respect at all times.

This community and the dogma on which the community rested proved to be remarkably resistant to the winds of change, often of hurricane intensity, that have been Western society's lot since the Reformation. Other communities, other dogmas, once equally proud and distinctive, went down one by one before the blasts of modernity. The university alone among the communities born in the Middle Ages remained strong; miraculously it seemed to gather strength, for in many ways its greatest affluence of spirit and prestige in the social order came in the twentieth century.

But its very affluence and prestige and power proved to be its undoing. Such was the yield to society of the university's resources within its community of teachers and students that it fell victim to that dread disease of mind the Greeks called hubris. Hubris is overweening pride, pride that must continually confirm itself through search for new glories, that must, Faust-like, seek the boundless and the infinite. Being noble, why could not the university be great as well? Being great, why could it not be wealthy and politically powerful? Why could it not be, at one and the same time, philosopher-king, philosopher-Croesus, philosopher-soldier, philosopher-statesman, philosopher-healer, philosopher-humanitarian, even philosopher-revolutionary? So might Faust have dreamed.

But it was not to be. The greater the university became, the less noble it proved to be in both purpose and bearing. The greater its external power, the smaller its internal authority. The wealthier in land, buildings, and income, the more impoverished in those spiritual and intellectual resources that had made the university perhaps the West's most cherished institution by the beginning of the twentieth century. A giant in self-esteem by the middle of this century, the university was already on its way to becoming a pygmy in fact; and, before long, the object of contempt, derision and hatred.

The university's enemies increased constantly in number and in strength. At first the weapons were battering rams, rocks, and torches. Then, in answering response, laws, police, and soldiers. All of this in a setting that had survived some of the most fearful wars, revolutions, and economic dislocations in history. The university had been able to repulse all of its enemies save those that its own hubris had created within its ranks. And when the dogma of knowledge and the community of mind that had been the university finally died, there was no one around to care very much. The university itself had seen to that.

INDEX

academic aristocracy, 73, 75, 81, 86, 105

academic bourgeoisie, 101–111

academic capitalism, 9, 71–87, 103, 104, 115–116, 119–120, 172, 175–178, 201, 219, 234; faculty radicalism and, 146–147; politicization as product of, 145–146, 221–222; sense of guilt accompanying, 166

academic community, 47–59, 239, 240; autarchical quality of, 57; code of honor in, 52–55, 60–61; essential authority of, 47–50; feudal character of, 60–67; hierarchy of, 50–52, 59, 74, 227; isolation of, 56, 58; search for, 171–196; sense of superiority in, 55–56. *See also* American universities; community; university

academic dogma, 24–40; academic faith and, 39–40, 42; aristocratic character in, 29, 187; knowledge and, 24–32, 41–42, 47, 116, 238, 239, 241; scholarship and, 30–35, 38–40, 59

academic entrepreneurs, 73–77, 81, 86–87, 101–102, 104, 147

academic faith, 39–40, 42

academic freedom, 16, 60–67, 222

academic gown, 16

academic litigation, 146, 149, 150

academic Protestantism, apostles of, 112–113

academic tenure, 16, 48, 60–67

Acton, John Emerich, 21

Adams, Brooks, 3

Adams, Henry, 3

administrative ability, 76–77

admission(s), applications for, 205; faculty authority and, 15, 48, 51, 214; pride in, 205

affluence, revolution and, 161–162

Age of Reason, 24

Agricultural Extension Service, 131, 190

agricultural institutes, 89

agricultural science, 26; departments of, 131

agriculture, American university service to, 15, 129–132, 192–193

alcoholism, 189

American Association of University Professors, 67

Robert Nisbet is a distinguished American sociologist and historian of ideas. He has long been associated with the University of California, Berkeley and later Riverside, as teacher, scholar, and administrator. He went to Riverside as Dean of the College of Letters and Science, and later became Vice-Chancellor there, but during the last eight years he has returned primarily to teaching and writing. He has been a Guggenheim Fellow and Visiting Professor at such institutions as the University of Bologna, Columbia University, and Princeton University. His writings include *The Quest for Community, Social Change and History, The Sociological Tradition, Tradition and Revolt,* and *The Social Bond.*